Human Capital in the New Legal Ecosystem

EDITED BY ALEX DAVIES

Commissioning editor
Alex Davies

Published by
Globe Law and Business Ltd
3 Mylor Close
Horsell
Woking
Surrey GU21 4DD
United Kingdom
Tel: +44 20 3745 4770
www.globelawandbusiness.com

ISBN: 978-1-78358-400-0
A catalogue record for this book is available from the British Library

Contents

Executive Summary

The COVID-19 pandemic has changed working practices across the globe. It has been predicted that as much as 80 percent of the legal workforce will remain transient or permanently working from home after the COVID-19 crisis ends, with only around a fifth as full-time office workers. Although law firms typically weather downturns better than the overall economy, revenues, working practices, and working culture will all change. The expected economic downturn may not directly translate into a decline for professional services, as market difficulties, regulatory responses, stimulus programs, changes in employment, and other stressors provide potential sources of demand – particularly in the legal sector.

What is clear is that personnel issues will come to the fore, and law firm leaders will have to respond proactively, both to mitigate risk and to make the best of a challenging and changing situation. Transitioning from an industry famed for office working to one that is more responsive, flexible and individualistic will provide as many opportunities as it will challenges, and those law firms willing to make the move to a more business-oriented model will stand to reap the benefits.

Our opening chapter, by Timothy B. Corcoran, looks at how the COVID-19 pandemic has exacerbated the need to recognize the different incentives that are required to allow lawyers to pursue different definitions of their highest and best use. Law firms have indisputably evolved into more complex businesses, and like all businesses, it requires a variety of skills and talents to run one effectively. However, too many law firm cultures recognize and reward but one contribution from their owners – billing time. Delivering legal services will always be critical, but other contributions have grown to be equally important. Developing and shepherding strategy, managing client relationships, managing lawyers and staff, generating new revenue streams, innovating to create competitive advantages, and managing daily operations are just a few of the tasks that law firm partners must take on, and not everyone is suited to these roles. In the new legal ecosystem, modern law firms must recognize and reward these meaningful contributions in order to remain competitive.

What is clear is that personnel issues will come to the fore, and law firm leaders will have to respond proactively, both to mitigate risk and to make the best of a challenging and changing situation. Transitioning from an industry famed for office working to one that is more responsive, flexible and individualistic will provide as many opportunities as it will challenges.

Economic pressures of the past decade have been forcing law firms, in-house law departments, and others to look for ways to improve the quality of legal services while reducing cost. The COVID-19 pandemic has accelerated those efforts. Chapter two, by Michael Roster, formerly managing partner of Morrison & Foerster's Los Angeles office, surveys ways to have junior lawyers functioning at mid- and even senior-associate levels; how to incentivize partners to implement more efficient yet more profitable staffing models; ways to improve client satisfaction and outcomes; and ways to restore high realization rates for law firms. Some might think this all is impossible. In fact, it's very doable, and those firms and companies that hesitate are going to be the losers in a rapidly changing legal market.

Seventy-five percent of lawyers do not think that the law is a service industry. This is the single biggest commercial issue for law firms. Chapter three, by Jon Whittle, challenges law firms to address the structural flaw that will prevent many of them building competitive, commercially successful businesses in the new legal ecosystem. Law firms need to know how to recruit, manage, and advance non-legal skills to help drive their business forward. For generations, law firms have been run by lawyers and in this chapter Jon investigates what skillsets are missing in many firms and, crucially, how law firms can incorporate the non-legal skills they absolutely need to thrive. Equally importantly, he explains how law firms need to address their culture and structure so that disciplines such as sales, marketing, HR, and customer service can shape the commercial direction of the business. Few other industries put commercial strategy solely in the hands of the people that make the product, and yet many law firms contrive to put 99 percent of the control in the hands of lawyers. Success in the new ecosystem will require this to change.

Chapter four, by Jennifer Johnson, CEO and founder of Calibrate Legal, and Erin Meszaros, chief business development and client service officer at Eversheds Sutherland, discusses the professionalization of business services talent. The world is changing and so is the talent needed for a law firm business services group to really rise to the next level. With the focus on innovation and change, it only seems right that you would build a team of diverse individuals who have in-house legal services experience as well as those with non-legal services experience. This chapter focuses on strategies to support the need for business services professionals from non-legal backgrounds to really maximize a team's efforts, as well as realize the benefit of bringing those non-legal and legal backgrounds together.

An organization's culture is an intricately woven fabric of values, standards, traditions, and behavioral norms. Each law firm has a unique culture, often one that has been inherited rather than actively shaped and directed. It is most easily defined, not by a vision statement or set of values promoted on the website, but how its people actually behave and how firm policies and leaders inculcate, reinforce or deviate from the behaviors of the stated culture. The COVID-19 pandemic has forced law firms to shift their operating models and to adeptly move to a remote work environment. This has had significant impacts on the way firms communicate with and support clients and employees, how work is completed and delivered, and has tested many traditional norms and assumptions in how law firms and partnerships sustain themselves.

Chapter five, by Susan Saltonstall Duncan of Rainmaking Oasis, includes the core components of law firm culture, how the pandemic has changed traditional models and culture, how to assess the culture you have, as well as approaches for improving your culture to compete in the future.

In 2016, the publication of two prominent studies of lawyers and law students in the US highlighted the disproportionate rate at which these groups experienced substance use and mental health disorders. In response, the National Task Force on Lawyer Well-Being published recommendations for addressing these issues and calling upon the legal profession to go from a culture of ill health to one that prioritizes wellbeing. Recommendations for legal employers, particularly mid- to large-size law firms, were incorporated into the WellBeing Pledge Campaign, an ongoing project of the American Bar Association's Commission on Lawyer Assistance Programs. Initial results from Pledge signatories demonstrate that many US and global law firms are adopting a variety of creative and comprehensive strategies to promote the wellbeing of their attorneys and staff. In chapter six, Bree Buchanan and Jonathan Beitner highlight some of the most exciting and innovative initiatives currently being implemented by some of the most successful firms in offices around the world, offering many lessons relevant to these challenging times.

Chapter seven, by Renee Branson, builds on this, looking at how COVID-19 has changed our understanding and prioritization of well-being in the workplace. The legal industry, in recent years, has begun to place greater emphasis on mental wellbeing, and the COVID-19 pandemic shifted nearly everything about the way we work, meaning the pursuit of mental health and resilience will accelerate. New challenges to our wellbeing emerged, and pre-existing ones were exacerbated. Renee begins by investigating the impact of this global pandemic on mental health, productivity, and cognition. She then answers the question of how to create a culture of resilience that mitigates those harmful impacts. Renee explores the various domains and skills that make up a resilient mind and, ultimately, a resilient organization.

Chapter eight then looks at culture from a generational standpoint. With so much attention focused on generational challenges in the workplace, asks Lauren Stiller Rikleen, president of the Rikleen Institute for Strategic Leadership, why have we still not reached a demographic détente? In the legal profession, the level of disquiet and frustration that exists between partners and associates can be higher than in other workplaces where there is a greater programmatic focus on talent retention and management. But the important tasks of strengthening client service and building a client base for the future is dependent on bridging these divides.

The generational challenges experienced among Boomers, Gen Xers, and Millennials may soon be exacerbated as future Gen Z lawyers come of age and enter the workplace. The oldest members of this generation are likely in law school, while the youngest are just beginning their grade school journey. All are experiencing the effects of a pandemic at a deeply vulnerable time, resulting in the disruption of their education and social development.

How members of Gen Z will integrate into the workplace is currently an open question. Their lost opportunities may have long-term effects on some aspects of their development, but they may also emerge with a deep reservoir of grit and resilience. The sustainability of any law firm requires that these strengths and weaknesses be recognized and addressed. This chapter explores the generational conversations that need to take place in an increasingly competitive profession. Building a future that is client-focused requires a greater investment in and willingness to understand the backgrounds and experiences that shape generational patterns. As with all relationships, opening lines of communication is the first significant step to developing a blueprint for successful growth.

For many legal businesses, the impact of COVID-19 has been felt most powerfully as a forcible shove into a new world of homeworking. As an accelerator, the pandemic has opened the gates to a new way of working that was perhaps already lumbering over the horizon. But are we ready to close the doors on the office? In chapter nine, Clare Harman Clark of Taylor Wessing discusses the fact that many lawyers are currently finding that it's less a case of working from home, more living at work – but the touted benefits of flexibility and balance are still tantalizing. If the future of work is to make the very most of this chance to rebase our working lives, is it truly possible to find a way of replicating digitally the collaboration and inspiration of the office that we miss out on at home?

The force of change for employees has been dramatic in recent months. The coronavirus pandemic has driven through new ways of working, with staff being required to respond and adapt in the moment. The ongoing threat of the virus, and the resulting economic downturn, has created uncertainty about the future, bringing employee relationships and employee engagement front and center, for both the immediate and longer-term. Research shows that organizations with actively engaged employees outperform across the board. To maximize performance and maintain a competitive edge, therefore, it is an essential component of business strategy, and is more important than ever. Chapter ten by Chris Marston of LawNet highlights the current thinking, as well as technical tips and operational examples from LawNet member firms.

Our final chapter takes the form of a case study. Chris Boyd, Allison Blixt, and Jullia Carretta collectively oversee professional development, diversity and inclusion, and employee engagement at Wilson Sonsini Goodrich & Rosati, and the case study demonstrates how the firm has adapted those to meet the logistical and human challenges of the pandemic and a fully remote work environment. The firm has taken a multi-pronged, collaborative approach to address challenges including moving everyone virtual, communicating and managing across 1,600 offices, maintaining wellbeing when work and home life merge, and connecting with colleagues and clients. Underlying all of these is a focus on supporting its diverse talent and developing additional D&I initiatives.

About the authors

Jonathan Beitner is an attorney, certified coach, and frequent speaker and author on topics related to attorney development and wellbeing. He helps attorneys identify and achieve their professional and personal goals, and works with firms, law schools, and bar associations to help their lawyers, students, and staff be more productive, happier, and healthier. As a co-creator of the American Bar Association's Well-Being Pledge, a lead organizer for the first annual Lawyer Well-Being Week, and chair of the ABA Commission on Lawyers Assistance Programs' Well-Being Committee, Jonathan has experience creating and implementing industry-wide initiatives to help lawyers thrive. Jonathan previously practiced as a commercial litigator at Jenner & Block LLP and clerked for federal judges on the Sixth Circuit and Eastern District of Michigan after graduating from the University of Michigan Law School.

Allison Blixt is director, professional development, diversity and inclusion at Wilson Sonsini Goodrich & Rosati, based in the New York office. Allison leads the firm's professional development and diversity and inclusion teams, strategies and initiatives. This encompasses lawyer and staff development, diversity and inclusion, wellbeing and engagement, legal training, and internal and client CLE programs. Allison has an undergraduate degree from Vassar College and a law degree from the University of North Carolina School of Law. Before joining Wilson Sonsini, she was a corporate lawyer in New York and London and then transitioned into law firm PD and D&I in London.

Chris Boyd is the chief operating officer of Wilson Sonsini Goodrich & Rosati in Palo Alto, California. Chris leads the firm's teams that handle attorney recruiting, business development, diversity and inclusion, human resources, knowledge management, marketing, practice management, professional development, research and information services, and work allocation. These teams work with firm and practice leaders to implement processes, programs, and tools that support the firm's business goals and help the firm deliver more value to clients. Chris has an undergraduate degree from Princeton University and a law degree from Stanford Law School. Before joining Wilson Sonsini's management team, he worked as a management consultant, corporate and securities lawyer, and technology company knowledge management leader. He is a member of the board of directors of the International Legal Technology Association and the board of trustees of the College of Law Practice Management.

Renee Branson is the founder and principal at RB Consulting. Combining 20 years in education, counseling, and non-profit leadership, her passion and purpose is helping individuals, teams, and organizations cultivate resilience. After years of working with survivors of trauma she now teaches others the skills of resilience for workplace wellbeing. As a certified resilience coach (CReC), she provides clients with immediately usable tools to increase resilience, wellbeing, and optimism in the workplace. She works with lawyers, educators, business professionals, non-profit leaders, and others to help them understand and incorporate resilience in their own professional lives and in the teams they lead. Renee is a member of the American Bar Association's Attorney Wellbeing Committee. Renee speaks to international audiences on resilience and wellbeing, including as a guest lecturer at the UCLA School of Law. She holds an MA in counseling psychology from the University of Colorado and a BS from The Ohio State University.

Bree Buchanan is founding co-chair of the National Task Force on Lawyer Well-Being and is a co-author of its groundbreaking 2017 report, *The Path to Well-Being: Practical Recommendations for Positive Change*. Bree is chair of the ABA Commission on Lawyers Assistance Programs (2017-2020) which works to ensure assistance is readily available for those in the legal community experiencing issues related to substance use or mental health issues. As director of the Texas Lawyers Assistance Program from 2013 until retirement in 2018, she worked with individual lawyers experiencing these issues, and with legal employers who were seeking resources and support for their staff. Her tenure with that program followed a two-decade legal career that included positions as a litigator, lobbyist, and law professor. She is now senior advisor with Krill Strategies, LLC, providing consultation on issues related to lawyer wellbeing and impairment for major US and global legal employers.

Bree is a frequent speaker for international and national law-related organizations, as well as global law firms on strategies for lawyer wellbeing and impairment. In 2018, she was awarded the "Excellence in Legal

Community Leadership Award" by Hazelden Betty Ford Foundation. She has shared her own story of recovery as a featured guest on podcasts in the United States and Canada.

Jullia Carretta is professional development and diversity manager at Wilson Sonsini Goodrich & Rosati in Palo Alto, California. Jullia collaborates with key stakeholders to develop and implement the firm's diversity and inclusion strategy and initiatives. She serves as a liaison to clients and external organizations dedicated to increasing diversity in the legal profession. Jullia has a bachelor's degree in Political Science, with an emphasis in Middle Eastern Studies from the University of California, Santa Barbara. Before joining Wilson Sonsini, she worked in recruiting and development at two other law firms. Between recruiting roles, Jullia spent some time adventuring in Korea, teaching English to young children and exploring southeast Asia. She is an active member in the Association of Law Firm Diversity Professionals, Corporate Inclusion Diversity Consortium and the National Association for Law Placement.

With more than 25 years of hands-on professional service experience, **Erin Corbin Meszaros** helps Eversheds Sutherland (US) attorneys turn business strategies into business successes. Through various firm initiatives she develops innovative solutions designed to enhance client satisfaction and increase brand awareness. Erin works one-on-one with attorneys on their professional and business development opportunities to help integrate and align their individual initiatives with the firm's overall business objectives. She also guides and supports practice groups and sectors to ensure the firm's strategic goals are met.

Erin's career includes numerous successful business initiatives, such as implementing and executing a firm's five-year strategic plan, implementing and executing a forward-thinking client feedback program, initiating and completing a re-branding campaign, conducting an in-depth client relations coaching program, and creating a unique customer relationship management (CRM) database course, which effectively increased firm-wide usage.

Timothy B. Corcoran is a legal management consultant with offices in New York, Charlottesville, and Sydney and a global client base. He's a keynote speaker, author, and legal commentator. Tim brings his deep experience from over two decades as a senior corporate executive to guide law firm and law department leaders through the profitable disruption of outdated business models. His disruptive, confident, and sometimes irreverent stage presence enables him to bring levity to topics of particular gravitas, while masterfully navigating tough discussions from a refreshing perspective. Audiences embrace Tim's simplification of complex concepts, his practical and actionable advice, and his deep understanding of both the psychology and economics of change.

As a change agent, Tim's focus is on helping law firms operationalize their strategy, improve profits with project management and process improvement, embrace profitable alternative fee arrangements, assess and improve partner compensation plans, design new financial metrics and dashboards, build effective operations, train current and future leaders, refine business development skills, and embrace technology. Tim helps law departments embrace performance analytics, better manage outside counsel, and improve business velocity. Tim also advises legal service providers on sales effectiveness and go-to-market strategy.

Clare Harman Clark is a senior professional support lawyer at Taylor Wessing LLP, building on a legal career that began with nearly a decade at Clifford Chance and a stint at Russell Cooke. Before retaining as a lawyer, Clare worked as a journalist and within a government press office, and still regularly publishes articles in national and trade press.

Jennifer Johnson prepares today's law firms for tomorrow's legal marketplace. She calls upon nearly 20 years of experience inside, and as a consultant to, law firms to deliver industry-leading strategy and executive search services. Law firms around the world rely on Jennifer to find sophisticated talent – impact players who will bolster their brands and bottom lines. Legal marketing teams rely on Jennifer for the tools and training they need to drive performance and ROI. As the driving force behind the Revenue Enabler movement, Jennifer is passionate about eliminating the "non-lawyer" phrase and mentality. She speaks and writes on the topic regularly, and she guides Calibrate Legal's consulting services and product development.

Chris Marston is chief executive of LawNet, one of the leading providers of specialist support for law firms in the UK and Ireland. Formerly with Lloyds Banking Group, where he instigated and headed the specialist division for professional practices, he also spent many years in commercial banking, working with owner-managed businesses of all sizes. Widely respected as a champion of innovation in legal sector leadership and a well-known voice in the sector, he lobbies on behalf of network members, which range from £2m to £25m turnover.

LawNet operates as a collaborative, mutually-owned national network where independent law firms access big firm resources and benefit from collective purchasing, shared knowledge, best practice and specialist expertise. There are currently some 70 member firms and a condition of membership is that firms achieve and maintain the LawNet ISO 9001 standard and associated Mark of Excellence.

Michael Roster was formerly managing partner of Morrison & Foerster's Los Angeles office, co-chair of the firm's financial services practice group worldwide, and a member of the firm's policy committee. In 1993, Michael was appointed general counsel of Stanford University, Stanford Medical Center, and Stanford Management Company. He subsequently was executive vice president and general counsel of Golden West Financial Corporation. Michael has also served as chair of the Association of Corporate Counsel, an outside director and vice chair of Silicon Valley Bank, chair of the Stanford Alumni Association, steering committee co-chair of ACC's Value Challenge, and chair of two start-up companies. He currently teaches Contract Drafting and Analysis at the University of Southern California Gould School of Law and is a director of MDRC in New York, a non-profit organization that evaluates the effectiveness of government and other programs affecting lower- and moderate-income families and individuals.

Susan Saltonstall Duncan has provided management and business development consulting to more than 160 law firms and professional service organizations and coaching services to nearly a thousand individual professionals since 1987. Her consulting firm advises firms, practice groups, and individual professionals on firm and practice/sector strategy and leadership, business and practice development, succession planning, client development, feedback and needs assessment interviews, lateral integration strategies, firm values, visions and culture, and innovation. She also consults and provides coaching to individual and groups of women, attorneys of color, and other underrepresented minorities.

Susan has been an innovator in the profession, having served as one of the first in-house professional development directors in the country in 1982, one of the first law firm marketing directors in 1984, and is a founding member of the Legal Marketing Association. In 2002, she launched a software version of her personal marketing planning and coaching system called RainMinder® – "Mind your business, grow it every day".

Prior to forming her first consulting business in 1987, Susan worked in two national law firms where she assisted in organizing efforts in client and practice development, communications and public relations, governance and planning, attorney recruitment, performance evaluation and training and paralegal management. From 2011 to 2012, Susan went back in-house and served as global chief strategy and development officer of a 1,250 lawyer firm with 37 offices in 17 countries.

Lauren Stiller Rikleen, founder and president of the Rikleen Institute for Strategic Leadership, is a preeminent provider of training, speaking, and consulting services to professional services entities, businesses, and organizations seeking to create an engaged, respectful, diverse, and inclusive culture. As a former law firm equity partner, Lauren managed an environmental law practice and frequently served as a mediator. For two decades, she was selected by her peers to be listed in *Best Lawyers in America*. She has also been included in Chambers USA *America's Leading Business Lawyers* and in *Massachusetts Super Lawyers*.

Lauren is the author of four books, including *The Shield of Silence: How Power Perpetuates a Culture of Harassment and Bullying in the Workplace*, and *You Raised Us – Now Work With Us: Millennials, Career Success, and Building Strong Workplace Teams*.

Lauren has served in numerous leadership roles within the American Bar Association, including as a member of the Board of Governors, chair of the Section of Civil Rights and Social Justice, and as a member of the ABA Journal Board of Editors. She currently is co-chair of the Women's Caucus and a member of the Standing Committee on Publishing Oversight. Among many other leadership roles in her community and profession, Lauren is a former president of the Boston Bar Association. She is the recipient of numerous awards, including the American Bar Association's Margaret Brent Women Lawyers of Achievement Award and being named by Public Media's Next Avenue as one of the 50 Most Influential People in Aging.

More detailed information about Lauren and her background is available on the Rikleen Institute website at www.RikleenInstitute.com.

For the last ten years, **Jon Whittle** has been working on the future of law firms, focusing on strategies and tactics that help firms build sustainable, competitive advantage. Working in a senior leadership role at LexisNexis he introduced cutting edge market research and thought leadership and is a recognized authority on how law firms can build and grow. He is also the architect and author of the widely read LexisNexis

Bellwether Reports, which now play an important role in shaping the strategic development of law firms. Previously, Jon worked for two decades delivering commercial growth, at board level, in some of the UK's largest media companies and he applies the fruits of this experience, successfully, to the world of law firm development. Jon now runs a consulting business and is particularly focused on helping law firms deliver commercial change with an emphasis on strategic development, successful project management, implementing new technologies, and evolving business operations. Jon is a specialist in building growth and value using market intelligence and customer insight. Jon is a regular speaker at legal conferences and seminars and is frequently asked to contribute thinking on the strategic future of legal markets.

Chapter 1:

Defining and rewarding a partner's highest and best use

By Timothy B. Corcoran

Let's start by tackling the oft-repeated maxim that lawyers are terrible businesspeople. This is true. But it's not always true. Lawyers are terrible lawyers. Also true. But also not always true. The first takeaway is that we have to stop the group-think suggesting that all who attend law school, pass the Bar exam, receive a license to practice law, and then actually engage in the practice of law, are alike. While there are certainly patterns of behaviors and personality traits that those who end up in the practice of law tend to share, these are neither requirements nor determinants of success. Particularly as the definition of success evolves. The greatest challenge in recognizing and rewarding successful contributions of lawyers in the modern law firm is the limited lens through which we examine lawyer productivity.

Confounding effects of academic bias

Anthropologists and sociologists have long recognized that humans are tribal animals, as prone to homophilic behavior as any other primates. We can manifest our tribalism in negative and destructive ways, as evidenced by toxic political debates, nationalism, and racism. We also gather as tribes in more mundane and innocent ways, say attending concerts of our favorite bands, buying the trendy fashion accessory, or strutting about in our favorite football team's colors on game day. Indeed, according to retail analysts, the market for team sports apparel – shorts and hats emblazoned with team names and logos – is expected to reach USD 24 billion by 2024! Tribalism is big business.

This same tribalism is clearly evident within the legal profession, as demonstrated by terminology in common usage such as non-lawyer, the Magic Circle, AmLaw 100, T-1 law schools, and more. But this mindset has left generations of legal professionals in the tight grip of a collective delusion that academic accomplishment is the single greatest determinant of success in a legal practice.

According to tradition, reaching the pinnacle of success in a legal practice requires a potential lawyer to accomplish all of the following:

- Develop excellent study skills as an adolescent sufficient to earn a high score on the SAT.
- Astutely identify and then gain admission to a leading university that serves as a feeder to leading law schools.
- Earn a high class ranking at a leading university and achieve a high mark on the LSAT sufficient to earn admission to a small number of top tier law schools.
- Earn excellent grades and high class ranking sufficient to be awarded a paid summer internship at a small number of leading law firms for each of two summers.
- Continue to earn excellent grades and high class ranking while also being recognized by faculty, e.g., earn a position on Law Review staff, sufficient to receive a full-time offer from a summer internship employer, or
- Be granted an interview and subsequently a full-time offer from another of the small number of leading law firms.
- Bill at least two thousand hours annually in whatever practice you're assigned while becoming an excellent legal researcher and writer.
- After several years of toil, receive an offer to join the ranks of equity partner, with a guaranteed annual income in the millions.

This journey is flawed. It has always been flawed. It doesn't require in-depth analysis to identify these flaws. It takes only a set of eyes:

- Top grades and high marks on standardized tests are known to reveal little more than an ability to earn good grades and score well on standardized tests.
- The definition of "leading" when referring to universities and law schools is dubious, given that many rankings value inputs, e.g., grades and test scores, rather than outputs, e.g., employability, alumni satisfaction, debt.
- The value of some academic distinctions, e.g., Bar Review, while notable, more accurately recognize capabilities as a legal scholar than as a practicing lawyer, which is not all that surprising given the role of law professors in awarding these distinctions.

- Many first-year associates leave their initial law firm employer before their fourth year.
- Most associates don't become partners, in large part due to a lack of business development skills and the resulting lack of business.
- Many of the biggest and "leading" law firms are losing revenue and market share to smaller firms, non-traditional providers of legal services, and clients who are increasingly keeping rather than delegating legal work.
- Aggregately in the United States, the average collection realization rate is 82 percent. This means that after all legal work is done and invoiced, buyers of legal services are refusing to pay fees they feel don't reflect the actual value of the work delivered.

The skills and competencies necessary to establish, grow, and sustain a successful law practice are only loosely correlated to the academic training and in-firm training that many lawyers receive. From the perspective of clients, whether individual consumers, the indigent, small business owners, or mega corporations, lawyers often lack, or consistently fail to demonstrate, critical skills correlated with client satisfaction. The good news is that these skills are in abundance in the legal profession. We just have to know where to look.

Unmasking the villagers

Let's break down the roles necessary to achieve success in a modern law firm. In many cases, people wear multiple hats. This is why it's even more important to know the hats, so we don't forget one or more.

Deliverer of legal services

This is the traditional role of lawyers. But it's also the role of paraprofessionals, many administrative professionals, and even technology. This isn't a new interpretation. It has always taken a village to conduct research, find templates and prior work product, write memos and briefs, complete and file forms and applications, and perform other administrivia necessary to package and deliver legal advice. Yes, of course, everyone is (presumably) supervised by a licensed lawyer, but that doesn't mean only lawyers are doing the work. Even though the dentist always pokes around your mouth for thirty seconds after a teeth cleaning, it's the dental hygienist who has done the bulk of the work. It's the same in law firms. Keep in mind, policies regarding the "unauthorized practice of law" are as much about erecting barriers to competition as they are about protecting client interests through some objective standard of quality.

Finder of clients

It's an extraordinarily elusive skill to find new buyers of one's services, again and again and again. Without this skill, solo and small firm lawyers would be returning to school to become plumbers – a profession they might be dismayed to discover also requires a combination of technical expertise and business acumen to be successful. However, most large firm lawyers can comfortably focus on the delivery of legal work because someone else in the firm is presumably focused on finding new clients. We hope.

Keeper of clients

If there's one glaring omission evident to every trained businessperson interacting with a law firm, it's that law firms haven't grasped the concept of client management or client experience. Law firms are notoriously run as a loose confederation of independent businesses sharing a logo and some overhead expenses. This means that clients must endure differential service standards and processes with every person they meet in a law firm, even within the same practice, within the same office, working on the same matter type. What law firms do without fail, however, is name a relationship partner, which can variably mean a lawyer who won the client decades ago, a lawyer who regularly works on the client's matters, a lawyer who bills little to the client but manages the team working on the client's matters, or a lawyer who performs none of these tasks but who, in a stroke of good luck and timing, inherited origination credit from a now-retired lawyer. Note that no law firm ever recognizes a "non-lawyer" as the primary point of contact for a key client… though many capably perform this job every single day.

Lawyer lawnmower

These are the many business professionals tasked with making life easier for the lawyers who pay their salaries. Like lawnmower parents who spend years removing all of life's obstacles from Junior's path, the "non-lawyers" in law firms exist to handle the tasks that lawyers are too busy or important to care about. Traditionally, earning the trust of an influential partner was as certain a path to career longevity as was technical competence in a specific discipline. But times have changed. Now law firms hire deep subject matter experts in finance, accounting, technology, information management, information security, marketing, business development, professional development, diversity, wellbeing, pricing, facilities management, and many more. And then promptly ignore them. Or treat their deep expertise as suggestions that non-expert lawyers are welcome to ignore while pursuing what makes them happy.

Lawyer deciders

All law firms need leaders, and many serve in firm or practice leader roles, tasked with keeping the profits flowing and managing the daily squabbles between smart people who are conditioned from an early age to believe they are nearly always right. While the central thesis of this chapter is that lawyer personalities vary, it's most common to see lawyers in this role whose management style is primarily "directing", meaning they dictate to others what to do, when to do it, and how to do it, leaving little room for autonomy. Curiously, lawyers crave autonomy. This is easily reconciled by the deciders, who believe being anointed to a leadership role means their autonomy to direct others supersedes the autonomy of others. At least until their term expires.

Helicopter lawyers

Partners are owners, and therefore partners must be in charge. While the rise of extraordinarily capable, and patient, business professionals is changing this dynamic, there are plenty of law firms in which a lawyer must be named to lead every function or task. These roles, such as finance partner, marketing partner, recruiting partner, partner in charge of the office move, IT partner, website redesign partner, and retreat planning partner, require no specific domain expertise. However, the lawyers occupying these roles are expected to swoop in and make battlefield decisions, override prior decisions, increase or decrease budgets, agree to or cancel sponsorships, select which law schools to visit, determine training programs, and much more – at least when they're not busy tending to their full-time practices. These roles are often grouped together in an effort to give multiple constituencies an equal voice. This is how compensation committees made up of a rotating membership can change direction from year to year based on what contributing factors matter most to those in the room, irrespective of what mattered last year, and marketing committees can delay the launch of a new website for years because they can't decide on which font is appropriate for the new tagline.

Ornamental lawyers

As with any random sample of contributors, there are those who excel and those who, let's say, excel less. Law firms, particularly sizable ones, are marked by a number of lawyers who serve no evident purpose. They're not busy billing work, so they fill their days directing professional staff. They're not generating work for themselves or others, but they're quite comfortable exerting their influence based on equity points gained a generation before. They may no longer be prominent in their practice disciplines, or their fields may have become commoditized, so they'll happily bill time to any type of file that crosses their desk, operating under the assumption that, as a partner, the quality of their work product is unassailable. Some become practice group leaders, and some of these contribute less to the practice than the oxygen generated by the potted plant in the firm's lobby. But they'll happily take the management stipend each year and rewrite any press release that fails to mention their management title.

And yet somehow it all works. Miraculously, law firms put forth reams of quality work product every single day with nary a client complaint. Clients large and small have ready access to experts with deep knowledge of the law, at reasonable prices. We know, of course, this isn't always true. While many lawyers generate quality legal work and engender client loyalty, more than a few generate billable hours with quality and client satisfaction relegated to a happy and occasional coincidence. For some, however, no amount of evidence will convince them otherwise. "Nothing you say matters," says the middle-aged partner at the partner retreat, unaccustomed to being spoken to as if he had something left to learn about his profession. "My clients are different and my practice is unique. Clients don't ever question my rates or my quality, and when they do leave it's only because of the bean counters in their offices who want lower rates." Positive change comes from recognizing that the business model isn't working. In fact, it's never worked all that well for all stakeholders, notwithstanding the immense incomes the model has generated for lawyers. But the clients are finally exerting their influence, and they've laid out a road map to success. It starts with chancing how law firms operate.

What gets measured gets... measured?

In most law firms, the most valuable currency is production. Lawyers who consistently bill a lot of hours receive the highest rewards. Partners who consistently bill a lot of hours receive nearly unlimited autonomy to run their practice in whatever way suits them, without oversight, and certainly without meddling from lesser lawyers in management roles whose own billable hour production is tragically lower. High producers generally leave each other alone, unless they're fighting over origination credit, the second most valuable currency in a law firm. The ability to generate a healthy book of business is followed closely in importance by the ability to negotiate credit for a healthy book of business, whether or not there is any contribution to actually winning the work.

This endless pursuit for production and origination credit, often referred to as a lawyer's "highest and best use", dwarfs all other lawyer efforts. The entire impact of these other efforts – managing matters, clients, and people, for example – are often relegated to a small "intangible" category when it comes to doling out compensation. These intangibles can be used to round up, or hold steady, the compensation of a producer who's otherwise having a rough year. Partners serving in management roles sometimes receive compensation that's a function of their production, which assigns wildly disparate value to the same role. In other firms, all practice group leaders receive the same stipend, despite immense differences in scope, complexity, and revenue. It's time to find a more rational approach.

Professionalizing the legal profession

Law firms are businesses. It's not debatable. So, it's time to operate law firms with modern, professional business practices. Re-inventing the entire business model is a lot to tackle, but we'll maintain our narrow focus on job design. Specifically, what roles should partners play and which of their contributions should be rewarded.

Producer

It is self-evident that law firms should employ excellent lawyers. These are the technical experts, the lawyers who can deconstruct an issue, research potential solutions, and construct a compelling argument. The more technically complex, the more elusive the subject matter expertise, the more commercially viable the practice is, the more value it has to the law firm. With increasing value, a measure for which age alone is a poor proxy, should come increasing compensation. Producers should be handsomely rewarded based on the relative value of their contribution. In some cases, such as when the expertise has such differential value, or the loss of this expertise would be so difficult to replace, a producer might receive an equity stake as a retention incentive. Otherwise, let's stop conflating the roles of valued producer with owner.

Sales originator

The relative scarcity of good business development skills means that those who can successfully and repeatedly win new client engagements should be rewarded well for doing so, particularly if partners choose to do this full-time. But it's important to distinguish between winning new clients and winning new matters from existing clients. Finding new clients is more challenging than mining existing clients, but nevertheless doesn't warrant lifetime credit. At a certain point, all clients become "firm clients" and sales credit is only given for new matter origination. Origination credit can only be earned, not awarded in a negotiation or inherited. A lawyer either helped win the work or didn't. Other contributions are rewarded elsewhere. Those who consistently win work for others (a critical requirement of an owner) and not just for themselves (an employee behavior) can earn an equity stake.

Client manager

It takes a combination of skills including technical lawyering expertise, project management, people management, budget management, and client relationship management to successfully manage matters and clients. This is a significantly under-recognized role in many law firms. The impact of this role is easily measured by client satisfaction, retention, portfolio expansion, matter profitability, and revenue growth. It requires training followed by clear expectations and accountabilities. A lawyer can't declare himself to be a client manager, and this role doesn't by default attach to the partner who won a specific engagement. The reward ensues to the person doing the job, and no one else. This critical role has such a short- and long-term impact on firm health that those who do it well may earn an equity stake.

Manager

Flat organizations, i.e., those without a middle management layer, are effective only on a small scale. In larger organizations, management is necessary to ensure clear communication of expectations, to provide training and resources and support to those doing the work, to constantly monitor the market for challenges and opportunities, and to regularly keep senior management apprised of operational performance. There's no such thing as an honorary practice group leader, or a title awarded to the most senior lawyer or most competent technical expert. It's a fundamentally different skill set to manage than it is to produce. For marketing purposes, we can fabricate all the fake "chairperson" titles we want but these have no bearing on actual firm governance. Practice group leaders are held accountable to performing the role. They are also expected to foster collaboration and self-motivation and creativity, and not simply direct the actions of others. Managers should be paid for their management duties, and this is a cost of business, not a function of profit sharing, nor some calculation relative to other contributions. Managers can certainly also serve as producers or rainmakers, but only to the extent that these don't interfere with management responsibilities. The era of awarding the title of practice group leader based simply on high production is over.

Firm leaders

These are elected positions from within the partnership to serve in a full-time, or nearly full-time capacity, running the firm. Firm leaders are focused on long-term strategy, hiring and supervising capable managers, allocating resources based on an ever-shifting set of priorities. While they must be action-oriented, they are not expected to take on day-to-day tasks of operating the law firm. They do, however, have an obligation to find and manage the subject matter experts who will, whether these are leaders of business functions or those managing practice groups. Firm leaders are always owners because one cannot be a leader without placing the organization's interests ahead of one's own interests. These roles are compensated based on achievement of goals and objectives, at a level that reflects market value and is sufficiently enticing that capable partners with the appropriate skill set will find it an attractive alternative to producing or selling.

Managing partner

This role is a subset of firm leadership, but with two additional roles – serving as the face of the firm, and spending more time on operational issues. The c-level executives will generally report to the managing partner, and as a consequence this role entails getting deeper into the weeds than other firm leader roles. After reaching a certain size, no law firm should operate without a full-time managing partner. The effectiveness of the partner occupying this chair should be measured like chief executives in other business lines: Can she walk into another law firm as the managing partner and be effective on day one? There are relatively few law firm managing partners whose authority stems primarily from competence as an executive rather than from earning influence and respect of peers.

Business managers

Discussions of law firms often overlook critical functions and key business roles as secondary. In reality, there are many capable law firm business executives whose market value far surpasses some of the lawyers they serve. So let's stop pretending that only lawyers matter.

And let's strike "non-lawyer" from our lexicon, as it serves no descriptive purpose.

Law firm leaders should invest time and energy into truly understanding the skills and competencies necessary to capably lead a business function. Let's stop substituting familiarity or longevity or – gasp – a law degree for domain expertise. No more CPAs without a day of general management experience appointed to COO roles where they'll manage a staff of hundreds; no more chief marketing officers coming from the ranks of unproductive partners looking for a safe landing as they glide into retirement; no more CIOs promoted from the help desk without a shred of understanding of cyber security; and so on.

Ask for assistance from recruiters, consultants, clients, or other law firms to define the roles and responsibilities of key business leaders, and then allow them to run their functions under the supervision of the leadership team. That is to say, every equity partner doesn't get a vote in their priorities or approaches to running their function. Partners without business cases to support their wish list should be told no, and management should stand behind the business leaders, so long as everyone is operating under the same strategic and operational priorities laid out by firm management. Leaders who have failed to establish priorities, or who fail to support business leaders in the execution of these priorities, are by definition not qualified to remain leaders.

Incentivizing the new normal

Surprisingly, determining the incentive structure for a modern law firm is not nearly as challenging as actually evolving the structure itself. If law firm leaders embrace the above and organize the firm and its partners so that everyone is focused on their own particular highest and best use – and literally this will be different for every lawyer in the firm – then the roles everyone accepts will be an important first step in defining the rewards to which they are entitled.

Producers should receive compensation based on what they've contributed. But metrics matter. It's not enough to bill hours, or to count cash in the door. The work must also be profitable. And every producer must engage in good fiscal hygiene, i.e., prompt time capture, billing, collections. We must also incorporate market value. An excellent producer who delivers a good volume of profitable legal work deserves a fine salary. But when this salary exceeds market value, i.e., it's less expensive to hire new producers, then the slope of future salary increases should flatten. For producers to earn significantly more requires them to take on new responsibilities. Risk and reward. It's their choice to do more. Or not.

But comfort doesn't have unlimited earning power, even in a law firm that grows every year. To access growing profits, one must take on new responsibilities and accountabilities, or become an equity shareholder, which is another way of saying take on new responsibilities.

Rainmakers should be rewarded based on the profitable delivery of the work they sell. Those who don't actually do the work or manage the work have less ability to influence profitability once the work is won, but they have great influence over profitability in how they sell the work, e.g., through creative pricing and staffing arrangements. Rainmakers live a life of great uncertainty, so the rewards are generally appealing. But if they want safety and continuity, they must wear other hats as well. Some may feel more capable selling a new engagement when they're involved in actually delivering the engagement. Yet others might happily avoid billing time ever again. What they both share is the realization that selling work is only possible when there's someone to do the work, so they will need to share the economic benefits with others. While rainmakers can certainly earn an equity stake, those who generate work only for themselves are not demonstrating owner behavior.

Client managers should be rewarded! Most get no recognition today. Rewards aren't a function of hours billed to clients, but they can be in part a function of hours worked to manage a client matter or relationship. There are other suitable proxies available to understand the relative impact of the role – matter profitability; repeatability of revenue; penetration, or working for the client across multiple practices or matter types; client satisfaction, measured objectively such as via survey results or subjectively by periodic interviews; and satisfaction of those working on the client's matters. Key account managers in large businesses often earn very high rewards given the critical importance of the role. Lawyers engaged in client management roles may earn an equity stake if their competence is in such high demand, particularly since their actions are generally aligned more to firm performance than to personal accolades.

Managers and leaders should be rewarded at a level commensurate with the economic impact their efforts have, up to market level. While those serving in critical management roles should be well-paid, it's unlikely these roles will earn the highest rewards in the partnership, unless those in management also wear other hats. It's not unheard of in business for top salespeople to earn more than top management, in the right circumstances. Firm leaders should already be equity partners. Practice leaders are almost always equity partners, but it's far better to install an income partner or even an outstanding senior associate as a practice group leader than to anoint an incapable equity partner who simply can't meet the obligations of the role.

Business professionals should be paid based on performance, at market rates. Some firms have a rule that no c-level executive should earn more than the lowest partner, but this is as absurd as paying rewards based on shoe size. These are fundamentally unrelated. Performance metrics will vary based on the role, but each should have clear expectations explicitly linked to the firm's strategic priorities. These priorities override individual partner preference, particularly when the business leaders' actions benefit the firm and the partner's actions benefit only himself.

Law firms as currently constructed and managed aren't completely broken. But they're suboptimal. There's no question that many law firms generate enormous profits and the partners earn far higher than the norm. What's extraordinary is how this is still possible given the many built-in inefficiencies, processes that could not be better designed for the sole purpose of depressing profits, and rewards connected to self-serving and firm-defeating objectives. Imagine the possibility that many law firms could increase profits by 20-30 percent, even in the face of increasing price pressure, by better embracing roles and rewards that allow everyone to pursue that which is their highest and best use. If your highest and best use is driving positive change within your law firm, your time has come.

Chapter 2:
The secret to profitability and professional satisfaction

By Michael Roster, formerly managing partner of Morrison & Foerster's Los Angeles office

A tale of two metrics

A recent survey of clients[1] reported that at least two-thirds of companies are asking for fixed pricing. Of course, the real numbers will vary by company and types of matters, but as clients and law firms move to fixed pricing, they will inevitably find that attorney expertise and stability are the keys to the law firm profitability as well as client satisfaction and retention. And even firms and practice groups that still largely bill by the hour are finding increasing pressures from clients about their total fees while also addressing increasing unhappiness within the firms.

Whether it's to address the need to shift to more fixed pricing or to otherwise deal with client and attorney concerns, I believe two metrics will become very important:

- Leverage (that is, the ratio of attorney timekeepers to equity partners); and
- Retention (that is, the percentage of attorneys who started at the firm six years ago and are still there).

In recent years, I have been telling general counsel and other in-house lawyers, assuming you've identified firms that have the necessary expertise for a matter and are in the ballpark in terms of price, these two factors tell you everything you otherwise need to know about which firm to select. If a firm has four, five, or six associates per partner, it means they are likely to put numerous overly expensive timekeepers on your matter, have not invested in training of junior lawyers, and have a business model that anticipates and even incentivizes a high turnover of lawyers. Worse for the client, that loss of lawyers is likely to be concentrated in mid-level associates and above, notwithstanding the knowledge and skills those lawyers have finally achieved.

Some of the most successful law firms, measured by both profitability and client satisfaction, have almost as many partners as associates, and several actually have more partners than associates. Likewise, these high performing firms often have a retention rate of 70 percent or higher, versus 20 percent for the highly leveraged firms. Built into the models of the high-performance firms is the early and focused mentoring of junior lawyers, putting these highly capable associates on the front lines early on, and elevating associates to partner sooner rather than later. Those business practices have additional benefits in law school recruiting, engendering loyalty inside the firm, and establishing a more forward-thinking mindset throughout the firm. Leaders of high-performance firms also no doubt have taken into account the fact that the all-in cost of recruiting each new associate typically ranges from $200,000 to $300,000 and up, and that's before starting to train them. To waste this expensive resource makes no sense for either the firm or its clients.

Law firm realization rates and client legal costs

In the early 1990s, law firm realization rates were typically in the 90 percent range. In recent years, law firm chairs and other managers have told me their firms were in the low 80 percent range and some were dipping into the upper 70 percent range. This reduction in realization rates was because clients were demanding significant discounts from the posted hourly rates, and even then write-offs were increasing because timekeepers were focused on meeting their minimum billable hours requirements rather than working efficiently.

High-performance firms that focus on expertise and stability should find they are achieving realization rates that approach and even exceed 100 percent. They should also find that clients recommend the firm to others, which is the best form of marketing there is. Firms should find that there is significantly improved professional satisfaction within the firm since the incentives will be on building professional skills versus cranking out hours, and with associates and partners again feeling a commitment to the firm, including for their own professional development.

How can realization rates approach or even exceed 100 percent? The goal needs to be for bills to reflect the value of what the firm did, not its cost of production. That, in turn, requires the firm and the client to discuss and agree on factors that would constitute value and for the firm then to be compensated for meeting or even exceeding these expectations while internally it is implementing ways to reduce the cost of production and increasing the value of what it produces.

As long as a firm's profitability is tied to selling as many hours as possible and to continue to increase the cost of those hours, it is working against efficiencies needed generally, and for fixed prices in particular. Firms that currently have a substantial mix of work at fixed prices as well as billed by the hour increasingly find a schizophrenia inside the firm. On matters billed by the hour, associates and partners know they will be rewarded by billing lots of hours, and it's on these matters they can meet internal billable hours requirements for the year, or other similar measures used by the firm.

On the other hand, for work where tasks, matters, or whole portfolios are being billed at fixed prices, the incentive on those same associates and partners is to produce a very high-quality product and service but as efficiently as possible.

With fixed price work, it also is essential that the firm and client stop using so-called shadow hours – that is, hours that might be reported by timekeepers even though the matter isn't being billed by the hour. Because if that's what both the firm and client will look at, even though they say the matter is at a fixed price, the only success for both sides is if the total shadow hours match the fixed price, since anything that deviates too much one way or the other will cause the client or the firm to conclude the matter was wrongly priced. But once shadow hours play no role, now the firm has an incentive to produce a superb legal product and service at an internal cost of production substantially below the price agreed with the client.

A major auto company for which I was outside counsel once told me that it took them 100 years to learn how to run the company. In the past, the designers and engineers proposed great looking cars with great performance, but at a high cost. So then the accounting and marketing departments kept pushing to cut the cost of the proposed vehicle until it finally penciled out. The result: a very mediocre car, SUV or truck. Now, the executives told me, the company starts by asking what price a consumer will be willing to pay for a particular type of vehicle. Let's assume $40K. Then the company decides how much profit is desired. Let's assume $6K per vehicle. They then tell the designers, engineers and others: build a great vehicle for $34K that will be extremely competitive in the market at $40K. Once the designers, engineers and others had such a target, they got very good at meeting and exceeding expectations, the company's share of market significantly increased, ratings of its cars by third parties likewise substantially increased, and profitability became much more predictable as well.

The same methodology is now needed inside our law firms. What's a competitive price of, say, defending a wrongful termination or selling a particular type of commercial property? How much profit is desired, on average, on a matter of that type? Now, how do you produce a great legal service within those parameters? Often the result will involve using project management and better use of document templates. Often it requires the involvement not of the cheapest lawyers, but lawyers who, in ten minutes, can give an answer that someone with less knowledge or skills might take several hours to achieve. Although an individual matter of that type might vary somewhat in what it actually costs to handle, if the firm is paying attention to its entire portfolio, the average cost of production of matters within the portfolio becomes the key metric to monitor. Which then leads to the process of continual product improvement: how do we do it better, at less cost of production, at still higher profitability, and with increasing client satisfaction?

As for discussions with the client about "value", there can be a wide range of factors. In some cases, it might mean doing a merger or the sale of a commercial property for X price. In other instances, value might mean having measurably better jury verdicts and/or settlements in a portfolio of product liability cases. Or resolving cases in measurably reduced amounts of time. Or having fewer cases and disputes of a particular type in the first place – meaning, keeping the client out of trouble, versus making money solely when the client gets in trouble.

How to accelerate associate training

A critical element in this business model is to accelerate the knowledge and skills of junior and mid-level associates. Let me illustrate with three examples.

When I was co-chair of the financial institutions practice at my former law firm, our group would monitor which types of matters were likely to increase in frequency and value in the next year or two and which were likely to decrease. For example, in some years we might anticipate a lot of bank mergers. In other years, a lot of enforcement actions by bank regulators. So we started to take our junior and mid-level associates and give them several days of focused training in what we expected were going to be major areas of our practice going forward.

To be more specific, we had a mid-sized bank client that was being threatened with a very serious enforcement action by its regulator because of the growing amount of non-performing loans held by the bank. The enforcement was threatened not only against the bank, by the way, but also its officers and directors. So we sent a third-year associate who we had run through what we half-jokingly called "cram school" to work on the bank's premises for several weeks, poring through the loan files and showing why the bank had appropriately underwritten the loans, monitored the loans and was effectively handling the workouts, case by case. After a week or so, the bank's CEO called me and asked how long this particular associate had been a partner. Why? I asked. Because, he said, his bankers were coming to him and saying that the lawyer was asking all the right questions, was writing his analysis of each loan file with great skill, and seemed to be almost as knowledgeable as they were about commercial lending. I told the CEO that the lawyer in fact was a third-year associate. "That's incredible," said the CEO. He noted that most of his bankers had 20 or more years in banking and, since they regularly provided banking services to lawyers among the bank's key customers, they knew that most lawyers were typically making three to four times what they made. Our third-year associate, the CEO told me, was someone his bankers respected and felt was adding major value to the project.

Here's another example. When I was general counsel at Stanford, we outsourced approximately 90 percent of our legal work to three law firms based on fixed-price portfolios. That is, a firm might have all of our tax, intellectual property, and hospital regulatory work, where the portfolios included both counseling and litigation and all at a fixed price. What we were trying to do was harness the expertise of the firms, not their hours. And that quickly proved to be what was delivered. Business units were getting the right answers, and fast, and the firms' expertise was increasingly keeping us out of trouble. To the point that after the first year of the project, our total legal costs (in-house and outside counsel combined) had been reduced by 20 percent to 25 percent and where, after five years, we found we had half the litigation we had the previous decade.

A third example is the advanced contracts course I now teach. The goal is that second- and third-year law students be at a second-year attorney level or higher in contracts by the end of the course. Virtually all achieve that goal and many exceed it. What's remarkable is, it wasn't hard to do. It simply required my teaching them the basics of a contract, then having them draft a contract on their own, then having them write a formal opinion letter interpreting an extremely complex contract, and then in teams having them rewrite a contract and present the work product to the rest of the class functioning as a hypothetical client. Many of the students report back a few years later that their law firms can't understand how they could be so far ahead as compared to their peers. As I said, it wasn't hard. It required simply mentoring the students and designing a progressive set of assignments to bring them up to the targeted level of knowledge and skills.

How to incentivize partners to be more efficient, more profitable, and (yes) happier

The other benefit of this model is to change how partners think about themselves, their work, and their firm. When the incentive is no longer how many hours a partner bills in a year, how many hours that partner is supervising, how many hours are in a practice group's portfolio, etc. but the measurements instead are based on profitability and client satisfaction, the partner gets to return to the reasons she or he became a lawyer in the first place. Yes, the partner wants to earn a decent income. But she or he also wants to become increasingly skilled in one or more practice areas and over time recognized as one of the best in those practice areas.

Again, incomes are obviously important, but through the years, I realized one of the most important rewards to me and my fellow partners was when an existing or new client called and said they wanted us to handle a matter. Think about this for yourself, and then think about it for your colleagues. Those calls are, as the MasterCard advertisement used to say, "priceless". Those calls are an affirmation that you and your firm are being recognized as among the best and that an existing or new client trusts you with their legal needs.

At the law school where I teach – and I hear this from colleagues at other law schools – the full-time faculty typically say the law firms aren't good at teaching or mentoring. I politely tell my faculty friends that one of the most rewarding parts of my time at my law firm was mentoring the next generations of lawyers. Much of what I do as a lawyer, even now, is the result of some extraordinary lawyers who hired and then mentored me years ago. And at least at that time, my law firm colleagues and I tried to do the same for the lawyers coming after us. That is, we inherited truly extraordinary law firms and legal practices, and our obligation was to make them even better – not just for us, but for those to whom we someday would transfer our practices and the firm itself.

When the partners are focused on the two metrics outlined at the outset of this chapter, I believe their own professional satisfaction will quickly be enhanced, along with the other benefits discussed. Some readers might say this is all very quaint and doesn't recognize the realities of the legal business today. I say in response, look at the firms and practice groups that are highly successful and look at the ones that aren't. Likewise, think about firms where there is high internal satisfaction, and firms where there isn't, often notwithstanding the high incomes the partners and associates might be making at those firms. If you look at what distinguishes them, I think you will find these intangible professional attributes are key. And then look at which firms are getting the highest client ratings and see if there isn't a correlation there, too.

Back to the future

Economic pressures of the past decade have been forcing law firms, in-house law departments and others to look for ways to improve the quality of legal services while reducing costs. The recent COVID-19 pandemic has accelerated those efforts. What I have described here are ways to have junior lawyers functioning at mid- and even senior-associate levels; ways to incentivize partners to implement more efficient yet more profitable staffing models; ways to improve client satisfaction and outcomes; and ways to restore high realization rates for law firms. Some might think this is impossible. In fact, it's very doable, and I believe those firms and companies that hesitate are going to be the losers in a rapidly changing legal market.

Reference

1. https://bticonsulting.com/themadclientist/2-3-of-clients-want-fixed-fees-why-your-new-matters-will-use-an-afa

Chapter 3: Why non-legal talent is essential in the new legal ecosystem

By Jon Whittle, Jon Whittle Consulting Ltd

> *"Seventy-five percent of lawyers do not behave like they work in a service industry."*

This is an interesting statistic that often divides opinion amongst lawyers but rarely surprises those who work with law firms. For some, the statistic is a shocking indictment and axiomatic of the problem that lies at the heart of the legal industry in the UK. For others it is a statement of the obvious – of course lawyers don't work in a service industry.

Some lawyers are adamant that the law is not a service industry and that their role as an advisor, an expert, an independent provider of advice and learning, should not be classed as a service. An illustration of this mindset comes from an incident at a mid-sized practice that was looking to increase its "customer satisfaction" performance. It was suggested that the firm could provide the facility for all their fee-earners to take credit card payments, should the client wish to pay directly. The managing partner interceded with the line, "Under no circumstances – we're lawyers not bloody shopkeepers". This is, perhaps, an extreme reaction but it does illustrate a mindset that percolates through some of the legal profession. It is a mindset that drives a culture that promotes legal proficiency over all other considerations. If left unchecked, this same mindset can create legal businesses missing critical skills that are essential in the modern commercial world.

The statistic above comes from a LexisNexis Bellwether research study that I conducted a couple of years ago and the actual question we asked was more nuanced. We asked the respondents (lawyers and partners in UK law firms) to rate the degree to which other lawyers behaved like they worked in a service industry. Overwhelmingly the sample said that the profession did not behave like it was part of the service sector. This suggests that lawyers like to think they, as individuals, are approaching their work like a service sector provider and it is the rest of the profession, with whom they interact, who do not behave as if they are working in the service sector. Put crudely, "It's not me that's doing it wrong – it's all the others". By definition, this means, in reality, the majority of law firms do not behave as if they are providing a service. Whatever they might think they are doing, they are not providing an adequate *service* to their clients.

If law firm clients are expecting a service and lawyers are selling something other than a service, then we have a problematic disconnect. In the old world of monopoly supply this did not matter – if all law firms did not conform to the usual behaviors of service industry suppliers then all were equally difficult to deal with. In the new world order, if law firms do not build the ethos, the structures and the processes of service into their business DNA, then they are going to fail.

The structural challenge

It is now common practice to point out that law firms, owned and run by lawyers, are running the risk of being left behind in the new world order. Whilst it is possible to find firms of scale that operate without any senior non-legal staff, most firms have incorporated non-legal skills into their operations and it's now not uncommon to find marketing, IT, HR, finance and administration specialists working within law firms. The challenge is not that firms lack these resources but that firms lack the will to deploy these skills effectively. In almost all circumstances the balance of power, the decision-making heart of a legal organization, rests exclusively in the hand of a management team composed exclusively of lawyers. This means that decisions about strategy, about commercial direction, about what the firm does or doesn't offer, how the firm sets itself up, how the firm goes to market, are often taken in an environment where non-legal skills are not just absent but are seen as entirely irrelevant.

In order to build a successful commercial law firm, we need to start with the business plan. In my experience, the business plans of law firms are often quite different from the business plans of other commercial businesses. Law firms focus on product (legal services) and tend to be light on market positioning, sales, marketing, and commercial projections. Starting from first principles and rebuilding the business plan can help law firms structure their operations in a way that promotes and recognizes the importance of non-legal skills to the success of the total operation. A good mission statement is the sum of the parts of a good business plan and a good business plan draws together several key elements that determine why the business can succeed. I would contend that many law firms need to invest more energy, time, and resource incorporating the non-legal elements of a successful business plan into their operations.

The company description

Most non-legal business plans start with a simple description of what the business is for. In headline this will include a mission statement and will explain, in basic terms, what the company does, why it exists, and why it is unique. I would challenge law firms to see if they can describe their company and its mission in a way that would pass the following test: Can you spot your own mission statement if all names and locations and other identifiers are removed? As a research exercise I took the mission statements of ten well-established, mid-sized law firms and took out the names, locations, and any other "obvious" means of identifying the firm. The managing partner from only one of these ten firms could, subsequently, recognize their firm's own mission statement from the list. Essentially, they all said the same things, there was nothing unique, and all described the businesses along the same lines.

If a law firm has a mission statement that sounds something like the following then I would suggest that the firm has a problem and is going to struggle to build a successful business in the new legal ecosystem.

> *"We work with our clients to deliver their business goals. Our firm uses state-of-the art legal services to support our work and everything is tailored to our clients' needs regardless of their size. We take our time to listen to and understand our clients' needs and ensure that they get a solution that directly matches their specific requirements."*

This mission statement could easily belong to any of a thousand different law firms. How can a prospective client possibly choose and how does the firm know where to invest or how to build a strategy for growth? Equally, how would they defend themselves from competitor attack? A good mission statement needs to be written in a way that enables a potential client to understand instantly what a firm stands for. Everything a firm does hangs, directly, from the mission statement – it defines the business and must be unique to the business. No other firm should be able to claim your mission statement as theirs. A law firm needs to be saying something about their business that is unique to them, that defines who they are and what they do.

Market analysis and competitive position

In a world of rapidly increasing choice, legal market deregulation, and growing client power, it is vital that law firms have a clear understanding of where they sit in the market. They need to know where opportunity lies and where threat exists. They must have a clear understanding of their strengths (and these need to be defined in relation to the market) and where there might be weakness in their total offering. If a law firm has not tested their business against these metrics, then they are exposed. Significantly, it is important that the firm tests all aspects of their operation against these metrics. All too often, firms measure their strength and their weaknesses purely, or even exclusively, on their own perception of the quality of their legal work. In essence, they only look at the product and neglect to think about the market in which they operate and what their competitors are doing. They also often neglect to look at non-legal providers of legal services as competition. Again, being able to take a holistic view of the market requires a view that embraces a wider perspective that that of the legal talent.

Management and organization

This is critical. A law firm where the lawyers are the only voices with power has a challenge. Lawyers represent only one element of a successful law firm and a successful business plan requires that all skills get appropriate representation. In the new legal ecosystem, it is imperative, therefore, that a law firm constructs a business plan and structures its management and operations around a suite of complementary skills. In all law firms, non-legal skills matter and are as important as the technical legal skills to the future success of the company.

The balance of the complementary legal and commercial skills should be determined by the nature of the firm. The firm needs to know what sort of business they are running and structure their management and operations accordingly. I would argue that law firms fall into three distinct categories, all of which require a different approach to the market and a different set of skills and operating structures.

1. Product-led law firms. Where the firm delivers its legal offering in a way that is different from the competition, is defendable, and would be recognized as distinctive by the clients it serves. Such product-led differentiation could be in the form of standalone technology or software, the use of AI or Big Data applications, integrations with other jurisdictions or disciplines. Anything where the legal service cannot be copied or replicated easily by a competitor.

2. Market-led law firms. Where the law firm serves a defined market niche or provides a legal service to a specialist audience. This often manifests itself in law firms that serve extremely specific industry niches, for example "legal services for vineyards" or specific legal niches, such as "employment law for the clergy". The defendable position here is not so much the legal service as knowledge of the market and the unique requirements of the client base.
3. Sales-led. Where the law firm's success is driven by some aspect of the "way" the firm works. This is the most difficult to define and, equally, the hardest to defend. Any USP that the firm may have is a function of the manner in which the firm serves the market rather than the legal advice it produces or the market niche it serves.

In my experience, the overwhelming majority of law firms are sales-led. Equally, in my experience, many of these firms, particularly those run by lawyers, will shout themselves blue in the face trying to persuade you that they are not. They will tell you that there is something unique in their legal service (the product) that differentiates them from the competition. Often the argument is that their experience and seniority offer a better "quality" legal service than that of the competition. Sometimes the argument is that they are bigger (and big is, therefore, better) or older (and therefore more trustworthy) or younger (and therefore more friendly). In most cases, under the lid, the legal service is essentially the same.

What steps should a firm take?

You need to determine what sort of business you are currently bringing to market and determine what sort of business you wish to be. Is your firm product-, market-, or sales-led? Review your business plan and test its strength. I'd recommend enlisting outside support, particularly if your firm is owned and run by lawyers. Being able to iterate a solid business plan that can withstand pressure testing from the market is a crucial step to then acquiring and embedding the resources needed to deliver that plan.

Be prepared to face some difficult truths and start from first principles. This does not require the firm to stop but it does require management to evolve its approach to doing business. It is self-evident that just doing what you have always done will not ensure survival in the new legal environment. This is particularly true for firms that have, previously, been shielded from the full-force of competition thanks to regulated access to legal services.

Some thoughts on non-legal talent

One of the sacred cows with which many law firms struggle to deal is the concept of vesting some control of the direction of the business to somebody who is not a lawyer. In a conventional, non-legal, business it is entirely normal for the management team to be composed of office holders with a wide range of complementary skills. Alongside executive and operating officers one would expect specialists in finance, HR, marketing, customer service, sales, product and technology. The management team work to balance the cost and benefit of each lever, recognizing that the whole is, by definition, greater than the sum of the constituent parts.

For some law firms this balance of skills and equality of representation is particularly challenging. It is often enormously difficult for firms to get over the hurdle that their legal advice is, actually, the "product" and that it is only one constituent part of the greater mix. Clearly, in all law firms, the greatest cost and the greatest benefit comes from the legal talent and the service this delivers, but that should not then dictate the business plan nor should it dictate how that plan is delivered.

Particularly in sales-led law firms the role that non-legal talent can play in the delivery of a commercially successful growth strategy is paramount. The only meaningful way to deliver the firm's mission statement is to focus on aspects of the business proposition other than the core legal advice. In this context, in the new deregulated environments, it will be sales-led law firms that are most vulnerable to attack by non-legal providers of legal services. If a sales-led law firm is able to effectively pull the levers of marketing, sales and customer service then it can compete with firms for whom these disciplines are already a core component of their business set-up.

In an environment where legal services essentially deliver the same benefits from all suppliers then it becomes ever more important for the marketing and sales functions to drive the business forward. Providing compelling arguments in favor of the service from a law firm requires a sophisticated understanding of the market and the requirements of potential consumers of legal services. It also requires a proactive approach to marketing and sales that is designed to attract and retain the target customer.

It is important to recognize that effective marketing and sales in law firms does not require specialist legal knowledge or an intimate understanding of the law. For the majority of law firms, marketing and selling legal services requires, first and foremost, an understanding of the potential client and an ability to talk, using the client's language, about how the firm can address their needs and requirements. The buyers of legal services, by definition, also buy goods and services from other suppliers. Most non-legal suppliers invest time and energy, cost and resource in developing and managing effective marketing, sales, and customer support operations. When clients encounter law firms that behave so radically differently from other commercial entities it is not surprising that they find the cultural fit so challenging.

Law firms have a tremendous opportunity to thrive in the new legal eco-system. The market for legal services continues to expand whilst the social and business disruption caused by a global pandemic will lead to increased demand for customer-centric legal solutions. Law firms that can deploy, effectively, the tools, skills, and business models that have been so successful in other professional markets will be best placed to serve this new demand.

Chapter 4:
Growing high-performing business services teams in law firms

By Jennifer Johnson, CEO and founder of Calibrate Legal, and Erin Corbin Meszaros, chief business development and client service officer at Eversheds Sutherland (US)

The world is changing fast, and so are requirements for talent in law firm business services teams.

In the past, most people in legal business services (whether HR, marketing, operations, administration, finance, or IT) grew up within the industry, and as such were highly adept at understanding the fundamentals of the law firm business model and partnership culture. Today, as law firms adopt management systems and innovative practices from the corporate world, they also need people with specialist skills to fill new or enhanced roles. Often this requires firms to round out their business services team with talent from outside the legal sector to optimize the team's efforts.

A diverse, high-functioning business services team with a mix of legal and non-legal backgrounds can have real benefits for a law firm. Managed right, such a team combines continuity and institutional knowledge with fresh ideas, broader perspectives, and innovative approaches.

But growing this kind of team requires attention and focus from business services leaders. People from outside the industry need leaders' guidance and context on how law firms operate, the politics and culture of the firm, and the business of law. Law firm veterans may need help in understanding the rationale for innovations and changes to business processes that new arrivals recommend.

Recruiting revenue enablers™

When sourcing candidates for open positions on any business services team, it's critical to cast a wide net. Far too often, law firms focus their search for business services talent on people who have previously worked in the industry. This limits the candidate pool and excludes talented, experienced individuals who, with a little training and development, would be well positioned to make a huge impact.

When evaluating candidates, look beyond core functional job skills, which are simply table stakes. You are, after all, seeking business professionals who will drive efficiency, innovation and sustainable growth. These impact players are more than "overhead". Their job is to deftly manage the business of the law firm so that attorneys can focus on their expertise of practicing law.

That's why, rather than the traditional appellation of "non-lawyers", we call these people "revenue enablers. Whether they come from the law firm world or another industry, revenue enablers share some common characteristics. They have sharp business skills in addition to technical skills – for example:

- They value outside perspectives;
- They aim for progress vs security;
- They possess high "EQ";
- They educate others; and
- They offer insights based on data and research.

To identify people with these characteristics, savvy firms are incorporating personality and behavioral testing early on in the interview process. These tests can be surprisingly quick (taking just a few minutes to complete) and ask questions about traits, drivers, influencers, and comfort levels, giving the interviewer a quick and accurate overview of the candidate's past behavior (which is the best indicator of future behavior).

Getting the right person takes time – which is why many law firms are partnering with recruiting firms to procure the very best business services talent in the marketplace. Such firms know the market, who the quality candidates are (both on and off the market), and how to sell the role to the right candidate.

Our advice is to fill your business services team with individuals who embrace change and become bored with the status quo – whatever their industry background may be. Revenue enablers who are driven by this quest face challenges with an open mind and remain calm and true to the greater purpose, even under adversity.

Onboarding best practice

According to recent research by SilkRoad Technology,[1] companies that have a well-defined onboarding process experience 82 percent higher retention of new employees than those that lack one. In addition, new employees in these companies are 70 percent more productive.

Most law firms recognize the value of structured onboarding processes to bring new attorneys into the organization. They know that a positive experience during onboarding will influence the lawyer's productivity, engagement, and loyalty for years to come. But can the same be said for new business services team members?

Here are some best practices for onboarding processes used by leading organizations across all industries. In the spirit of continuous improvement, we suggest that law firms consider how these practices could be applied to current onboarding programs for business services teams.

Create a great experience

Onboarding processes are often evolved rather than designed. Over time, this evolution creates unnecessary complexity and results in a confusing experience for the employee. In fact, research[2] indicates that a typical onboarding process requires the employee to complete 54 distinct activities. Try starting from a blank slate – look at your current onboarding process from the employee's point of view. Look for redundant and out-of-order tasks, poorly written documentation, and instructions that are unclear, then re-design the experience from beginning to end using technology and modern online learning principles to create a high-quality, repeatable process. In fact, some leading companies are "gamifying" the onboarding process to create a fun, memorable experience in which new employees discover the information they need, rather than having it force-fed.

Provide business context

Too often, onboarding programs focus mainly on the administrative aspects of starting the new role – computer setup, network access, organization charts, timesheets, approvals, etc. Be sure your firm's onboarding process also includes information on the business of the firm, including its strategy and how it makes money. This is especially important for members of business services teams, who are often so focused on their own roles that they lose sight of the larger business context.

Encourage collaboration

The best onboarding programs motivate employees to make their own connections within the organization and start collaborating with peers as quickly as possible. Some companies encourage this by holding periodic onboarding events, where new recruits meet to share insights and experiences, and hear contextual presentation from department heads, technical specialists, and business leaders. Others create scavenger hunt-like quizzes that encourage new employees to meet with key stakeholders in the organization to uncover the information they need. Many companies are leveraging online collaboration channels like Slack to encourage collaboration from day one.

Involve the right people

An onboarding process does not run by itself – it requires care and feeding from the people who manage new recruits. This is especially true for business services talent in law firms. Because most new hires are attorneys, the core new-employee onboarding experience tends to be lawyer-centric and may not include information and context that is critical to business services teams. Involving business service leaders up front in the design of the onboarding program will ensure that the requirements of business services teams are included. Also, hiring managers need to have a role in the process. Leading companies provide hiring managers with just-in-time onboarding checklists of tasks that hiring manager need to carry out themselves – for example, lining up a peer coach, scheduling check-in meetings, etc.

Practice continuous onboarding

The best onboarding processes intersect with the firm's learning and development strategy – a new employee will move seamlessly from the onboarding experience into an individualized learning path. Leading companies ask new employees to define specific career objectives and help them create development plans to get there. While this can be difficult for business services roles (as law firms invest mainly in training lawyers) it is important to plan for the learning needs of new business services team members as they join the firm.

Consider the virtual experience

Onboarding becomes even more of a challenge when new business services employees are working virtually and don't get regular "face time" with their team members and the attorneys they serve. It's all too easy to overlook the needs of a new person when they are not visible in the office. For that reason, managers need to pay close attention to new employees' virtual experience of the firm. First, ensure that they have the necessary technology and training to engage successfully in online meetings. Managers should set up a schedule of virtual checkpoints to replace the face-to-face interactions that new employees normally experience. For a new employee's first meetings with attorneys, adopt a buddy system so that an experienced employee is always on the line with new person.

Cultivating intellectual curiosity

Your people represent all the intellectual capital and knowledge-ware that exists within your law firm. Through that lens, attorneys and business services professionals alike are both your largest asset and the key to your advancement.

The business case for investing in people seems clear, and virtually all law firms dedicate large budgets for professional development programs for their attorneys. However, most have not made similar investments in learning for business services professionals, and this is certainly a deficit that needs to be addressed.

Beyond formal learning programs, firms need to foster intellectual curiosity for all their people. When they do this, they open the door for untapped potential to flow freely. Encouraging intellectual curiosity requires intentional behavior changes that will cumulatively create a culture of continuous learning and development. This is especially critical in fast-paced, high-intellect disciplines like law. Intellectual curiosity is an individual's drive and desire to invest time and energy into learning more. Every person is born with intellectual curiosity, but this trait can become buried if not nurtured and practiced.

When someone is intellectually curious, they push to find the answers to "why?" and "why not?" The degree of intellectual curiosity is the intensity and persistence to go below the surface and ask probing questions to arrive at the core issues surrounding a particular concept. The ability to offer an original perspective is the welcome distinction many firms are looking for to gain a competitive advantage, and to encourage top talent to stay. How do you foster this within your business services team and culture?

First, model the behavior. Ask others what they think (including the quiet introvert) and then stop to listen and incorporate the feedback. When others see that the group's feedback is welcomed and useful, they are more likely to offer it unprompted.

Ask good questions. A key trait of successful leaders is their ability to ask really good questions. The best leaders foster this trait in others by encouraging their people to thoroughly think through an issue. They lead others with probing questions rather than telling them the answer, which stimulates deeper learning, research and thought. You may be surprised with what your team can come up with when given the chance.

- Challenge your team with "why?" and "why not?" questions. This cuts through the politics and the "we've always done it this way" default responses.
- Create an environment where it's OK to fail. This is rarely easy in a law firm but can be done effectively within the relative safety of a team.
- Put a reward and accountability structure in place that promotes turning ideas into results. Ideas without execution don't really add value.

Fostering a culture where intellectual curiosity is regularly modeled, practiced, and rewarded, builds an agile environment where innovation and progress can thrive, and impact players can be unleashed.

Mentoring

Research shows that the mentor–mentee relationship can add huge value to an employee's career. In one study[3] of sales and marketing professionals, for example, employees who were part of a mentoring relationship were found to have significantly higher engagement scores than employees who were not.

Most law firms law understand the value of mentoring for their attorneys – but high-potential business services professionals need mentoring too. While there's generally no shortage of possible mentors for attorneys in a law firm, the same cannot be said for the business services side of the house. In most firms, the hard work of mentoring these professionals tends to fall to a small number of business services chiefs, whose time and availability for the job is limited. As a result, far too many high-potential business services people don't get the benefit of mentoring at critical points in their careers. Expanding the mentor population for business services team members can help. This can be done in several ways, including:

- Expect business services staff to take on mentorship roles as they progress to more senior roles. Mentoring in itself can be positioned as part of an employee's development path.

- Enlist selected attorneys as mentors – those who understand the key role that business services teams play in the firm and are willing to contribute their wisdom to further the cause.

Mentoring relationships for business services professionals need to be seeded in an intentional and focused way to ensure best fit. Start with the business objectives you are trying to achieve in business services, and then identify the competencies and skills that are most relevant to those objectives. Then, organize pools of mentors and mentees who meet the skill requirements, using an application process for both.

You'll need to screen potential mentors and mentees to ensure they have the right characteristics and attitudes to benefit from the program. Consider the following screening criteria:

For mentors	For mentees
• Demonstrated empathy and honesty. • Ability to strike the right balance between criticism and encouragement. • Active listening skills. • Ability to help mentees set career goals and map development paths. • Willingness to commit time for mentoring conversations and check-ins.	• Demonstrated leadership potential. • Maturity and self confidence. • Openness to receiving feedback – whether praise or criticism. • Clarity about personal and career goals. • Willingness to commit time for mentoring conversations and check-ins.

To match mentors with mentees, you can use a facilitated approach (where an HR team member makes the introduction) or encourage self-matching (where mentees and mentors line up on their own). Whatever approach you choose, there must be systematic follow-up to ensure that relationships are established.

Both mentors and mentees need guidance and support to fulfill their roles. Leading companies have documented formal expectations for their mentoring programs, and provide access to resources, such as workshops and webinars, that are focused on mentoring skills development.

Mentoring is possible in a virtual environment – in-person meetings are not essential to a mentoring relationship. In fact, employees who work virtually need good mentors even more than those who work in the office. Encourage both mentors and mentees to use online meetings when face-to-face is not an option.

Developing business acumen

Many law firms struggle with developing business acumen in their business services teams. In fact, the most common complaint from attorneys about business services professionals is "they don't understand our business".

Why is this? These employees may be very capable and effective in their functional roles, but often do not have a formal business education, or understand how the firm makes money. They do not see their work as part of a larger ecosystem that contributes to the firm's success. As a result, they are not equipped with the judgement needed to make decisions and take actions that can significantly impact the firm.

Here's a simple example. A firm's administrative team made it a priority to reduce the cost of events held in the firm's office. In a cost-saving move, they created reusable elevator lobby signs to direct visiting clients to the events (rather than printing new signs for each event). While they succeeded in reducing printing charges, the reusable signs quickly became tattered and ugly, negatively affecting clients' impressions of the firm's brand as they arrived.

Another firm's marketing and IT departments were charged with acquiring a CRM system. They selected a solution that was very capable and feature rich – with no input from the attorneys who were supposed to use it. When the system was rolled out, attorneys were put off by its complexity – it did not match their business needs. The system (and the time cost of implementing it) was written off after one year.

Lack of business savvy can have other effects. It can result in decreased employee engagement, leading to higher turnover. When business services employees don't understand the big picture, their ability to provide practical input is constrained – the firm misses out on ideas that could improve operations.

How can law firms encourage the development of business acumen in their business services teams? Below are five essential approaches.

Provide basic training on the business of law

Every law firm needs a readily available training module aimed at those who are new to the legal world. The training should focus on the business of the law firm – who the clients are, how the firm makes money, what factors affect profitability, and the respective roles of lawyers and business services departments. At the end of the training new hires should have enough knowledge of the law firm business model to understand where their roles are expected to contribute.

Share the firm's strategy and goals

Some firms treat their strategic plan as a confidential asset – only a select few partners may even be aware that it exists. But the true power of strategy is unleashed only when it is widely shared throughout the firm. Business services teams need to understand what the firm wants to achieve in order to align their personal goals and make the right decisions in their day-to-day work. Business services leaders should be equipped to communicate the strategy to their teams, and to facilitate discussions about how each team (and individual) can contribute.

Cross-train business service teams

Functional specialists often focus deeply on their jobs and lose sight of the larger picture of the firm. In particular, they may not understand the interplay of their work with colleagues and other business services departments or attorneys. Over time this creates silos that reduce the quality and efficiency of a team's work. To overcome this tendency, invest time in cross-training specialist roles. For example, an IT help desk manager might spend a day shadowing a marketing or finance team member, to help them understand their daily changes with IT systems. A marketer could spend time shadowing an attorney – not to carry out a marketing task, but to obtain knowledge on how the attorney works. Another approach leverages regular team meetings – for example, a finance director could deliver a guest presentation about their job at the monthly meeting of the HR team.

Put the client at the center

Even if business services teams are not client facing, they need to see themselves as part of the firm's value chain to deliver a great client experience. For example, every team needs to know who the firm's key clients are. They should be aware of the client's ongoing touchpoints with the firm – from intake to billing – and how their jobs influence those touchpoints. Managers should reinforce this concept during individual and group meetings – every business team member needs to understand how their role makes a difference to the client.

Make business acumen part of performance management

Incorporate business acumen into your competency model for business services professionals. This requires defining the elements of business acumen that the firm needs, and then working with employees to set matching performance goals. Managers can then use performance reviews to highlight situations where an employee has demonstrated business acumen, and provide guidance on learning opportunities to increase their overall business knowledge.

"Stay interviews"

Many organizations ask people their reason(s) for leaving during exit interviews, but don't make a concerted effort to figure out why talented people choose to remain with the organization. "Stay interviews" with high performers should be part of every manager's toolkit. When executed correctly, stay interviews have the potential to help law firms retain their most talented business services professionals, and understand how to use them at their best and highest potential. Considering the future return on investment and competitive advantage of retaining your top people, it's valuable to understand firstly how to engage in these conversations and then how to incorporate this feedback into your firm's engagement strategies.

The process must be a thoughtful one, with support from the top down, and must represent the culture and engagement that your firm seeks. It's also important to have some structure in place for these conversations so that the process can be repeated regardless of the parties involved and to ensure that the feedback remains constructive and focused.

Simply Googling "stay interview questions" will provide you with an immense amount of recommended questions that managers can and should ask during a stay interview. These resources may help you personalize and develop questions to ask your direct reports and to gain a better understanding of the differing views on the topic. Managers can adapt these questions to their own style and customize their application to appropriately reflect the individual relationship with each direct report.

To serve its ultimate purpose, the feedback you receive should be met with a true willingness to hear it and consider the value of integrating some of that knowledge into your workplace. Using that information to inform future decisions sends a message that you listened and really care. Of course, you will not always be in a position to say "yes"; however, this type of ongoing feedback loop provides an environment where you can explain why not, or why not *now*.

Building an inclusive culture

In far too many law firms, business services professionals are not treated as full, contributing members of the team. In these firms, there is a clear delineation between attorneys and staff. Top rewards, perks, recognition, affinity groups and other programs are available only to attorneys.

Treating business services professionals as second-class citizens is not a sustainable strategy for law firms. These professionals are already sensitive to their positioning as outsiders within their firms and are becoming even more aware of this as time marches on. If things do not change, they will vote with their feet and opt to work somewhere they are valued and included.

Law firms should attempt to create a one-team culture where the diverse contributions of all members will be valued. Here are some actions to help you get started.

- Surface the issue. Survey or interview your firm's business services professionals to understand aspects of your firm's culture that may cause them to feel excluded.
- Review your firm's current programming for employees. For example, look at alumni programs and affinity/resource groups to see whether business services professionals are being unnecessarily excluded.
- Measure diversity in business services. If you have a program in place to track the diversity of your lawyer population, consider extending it to cover business services professionals.
- Evaluate your firm's benefits programs. Look for situations where business services professionals may not be treated equitably. Where warranted, be prepared to make cash investments to rectify those situations.
- Consider your firm's training programs. Do they include business services professionals? If you're already offering training on business skills to your lawyers, think about how business services teams could also benefit.
- Study your leadership teams. Leadership teams are where important business decisions are made in your firm. Do your most senior business services professionals truly have a voice with those teams? Expect firm leaders to exemplify universal inclusion by seeking input from, and providing mentorship to, high performing team members – whether or not they are lawyers.
- Think about your talent pipeline. Ask whether you are really getting access to the best candidates available. Many firms require all candidates for business services position to have prior law firm experience – this requirement excludes candidates who may have better, more relevant experience in other sectors, and creates teams that are entrenched in their thinking.

Over time, treating your business services professionals as valued team members will help your firm to attract and retain the most talented people, thereby improving innovation, performance, and business resilience. All in all, achieving the goal of universal inclusion will be worth the effort.

References

1. SilkRoad Technology/The Harris Poll, *US Trends and Applications in Employee Onboarding*, 2019
2. *Ibid.*, 2019
3. Sange and Srivasatave, *Employee Engagement and Mentoring: An Empirical Study of Sales Professionals. 2012*

Chapter 5:

Culture as an essential component of your firm's future health

By Susan Saltonstall Duncan, Rainmaking Oasis

Introduction

An organization's culture is an intricately woven fabric of values, standards, traditions and behavioral norms. Each law firm has a unique culture, often one that has been inherited rather than actively shaped and directed. It is most easily defined not by a vision statement or set of values promoted on a website, but how its people actually behave and how firm policies and leaders inculcate, reinforce, or deviate from the behaviors of the stated culture.

The coronavirus pandemic has forced law firms to shift their operating models and to adeptly move to a remote work environment. This has had significant impacts on the way firms communicate with clients and employees, how work is completed and delivered, and has tested many traditional norms and assumptions about how law firms and partnerships sustain themselves.

The convergence of the pandemic and resulting economic fallout, together with the murder of George Floyd in May 2020, other racial incidents and racial injustice protests, have created substantial stress of both a commercial and human nature, in law firms of all sizes. These crises have forced firms to examine how they operate and what they stand for. In order to benefit from the silver lining this disruption has created, firms should actively examine their cultures and redefine with intentionality the meaning of their partnerships, their vision, values, and operating procedures in order to be the kind of organization that focuses on the health, wealth, and wellbeing of its clients, employees and partners, and broader communities.

The core components of law firm culture

A firm's vision and values define its culture. Partners, employees, and other stakeholders who align with the firm's culture tend to foster a more productive and positive work environment, which improves recruitment, retention, productivity, and profitability. Those who do not adhere to the culture's behavioral norms and values often create friction, a toxic work environment, and often detract from productivity and profitability. Many of the characteristics that contribute to a healthy culture revolve around how employees are treated, respected, developed, compensated, and managed.

There are five primary components of organizational culture in a law firm:

1. **Vision, strategy and client service philosophy.** This represents a clearly articulated vision, mission and roadmap for what you want the firm to be, and how it will deliver services to and serve clients and the community. It is an articulated, shared purpose of why the firm exists and the role that people and processes play in helping the firm execute on its vision.
2. **Values and norms**. These are the beliefs and principles that the firm's stakeholders live by and follow. They are converted into policies and practices that are implemented, monitored, measured, and reinforced. They can be seen in rituals, firm stories, and lore and are observed in daily interactions with colleagues, clients, and communities. Diversity and inclusion are reflected in a firm's values and protocols.
3. **Talent development and management**. Culture is defined and exhibited in the ways its people behave and by the values, norms, processes, and protocols established to manage talent throughout the talent lifecycle. The human capital component of culture is represented in recruiting, training and development, employee engagement, attrition, diversity, knowledge sharing, performance assessment, advancement and promotion, rewards and recognition, communication styles and channels, leadership development, and succession planning.
4. **Governance and leadership.** This is the way the firm manages itself and is reflected through leader behaviors, decision-making composition and execution, how employees operate within the organizational structure, and how those in non-leadership positions access and influence leaders in the firm.
5. **Collaboration, trust, and respect**. This represents how people in the firm interact with and relate to each other. It includes how lawyers treat each other and those in other roles and stature, how

people work in teams and across functions, how credit and recognition are shared and how and how often all employees and partners interact socially.

How recent world events have changed traditional models and culture

The pandemic has created major disruption in the way law firms operate, including remote working, virtual interaction and relationships, and a reliance on technology tools for work delivery and team collaboration. Some firms have been forced to put conservative economic measures in place, including furloughs and layoffs, which inevitably create anxiety, distrust, and anger or resentment. These types of disruptive effects can put even the strongest cultures to the test.

Perhaps the most significant impact the pandemic has had on all businesses but certainly on law firms has been the need to focus on people – their psychological wellbeing and their needs. Clients and law firm leaders have come to realize what is important in their own personal lives, i.e., family health and safety. As one partner in a global firm put it, "COVID has put us all on a level playing field across roles and stature where we all are human and struggling with the same stress and challenges".

Because firms are operating remotely and have not been able to rely on the camaraderie and natural social interaction that comes from physically being together in an office environment, they have had to create alternative modes to help address the stress and anxiety of employees, the need for connection, and opportunities to be collaborative on work or non-work related activities. Even when this pandemic ends, many firms are likely to continue to allow remote and flexible work schedules and locations. The psychological challenges that leaders, partners, and all employees have experienced as a result of the pandemic have resulted in new approaches taken by human resources and talent and wellness professionals to help develop new skills and mindsets for creativity, innovation, and curiosity, including the safety to try new things, and resilience.

For a few years prior to the pandemic, businesses were called to action by the #MeToo movement, bringing heightened awareness to gender equality disparities, conscious and unconscious bias, and inequitable opportunity impediments. Firms have made some advances in this area, with efforts to promote more women into leadership roles, re-examine opportunities provided for client succession and assignments, develop flexible work and advancement policies, and address non-compliant and discriminatory behaviors.

Three months into the COVID-19 pandemic, the US saw protests break out in the wake of the murder of George Floyd and numerous other racial incidents between Black Americans and police officers. These events triggered outrage in much of America, which spread to other countries. Individuals and organizations began scrutinizing systemic racism and racial injustice. Law firms committed their resources of money, time, and talent to initiatives and groups to address and improve the policies and culture that feed or tolerate these injustices. These have sparked renewed interest in taking a close look at the policies and practices that firms must modify to build more inclusive and diverse cultures.

How to assess the culture you have

Many law firm cultures are inherited, not intentionally designed and nurtured. The way people behave, what they value, what is rewarded, and what is tolerated are all indications of culture. In order to ensure that a firm's culture operates as the positive, productive work environment it wants to have, a firm should undertake a thorough assessment of what the culture currently is. Recent events, especially the impact of working remotely/shelter-in-place and racial and gender inequalities, has exposed some serious weaknesses in many firms' cultures. This presents both an opportunity but also a mandate that firms consider what their cultures are and how they want to improve them.

Assessing firm culture can be done using digital surveys with owners (partners), employees, clients, and vendors. Those should be supplemented with focus groups and individual interviews as well as analysis of firm policies, client service and work standards, recruiting, training, compensation programs and other decision-making and operational procedures. In looking at the five core areas that comprise culture, the following areas and considerations would be helpful to explore.

Vision, strategy, and client service philosophy

One of the first indicators of whether your strategic vision is well-defined is whether every partner and employee can articulate it if asked. Partners and employees who believe in the firm's mission and reputation will reflect their commitment to it by how consistently they work to contribute to the firm's success. Firms often find it challenging to determine whether all practice areas and offices are of equal value or whether they should begin to prioritize resources based on market need, the competitive landscape, and profitability. While firms are reluctant to do so for fear of hurting lawyers' feelings, it is important to honestly assess in what areas the firm is particularly strong or weak and which areas or skill sets are viewed as fungible legal services. This may impact how the firm allocates resources, does hiring, or even spins off less profitable practices. Despite being a sound business practice, firms often avoid this approach for fear it may erode its culture of trust and respect.

A firm's mission should reflect both internal and external factors. When assessing this cultural component, consider whether the firm is driven by market trends and most importantly, by client needs, or is strategy developed by "gut" reactions of partners and internal factors and metrics. A reflection of how committed a firm is to being client-focused is how and how frequently the firm measures and acts upon client satisfaction and feedback. A firm's commitment to innovation, whether the firm has the most efficient and up-to-date technology to support client work, and how it utilizes process improvement, project management resources, and alternative staffing to maximize efficiency and cost-effectiveness, all reflect firm culture.

Values and norms

Values and norms are best evaluated by looking at behaviors and policies. The firm may espouse certain values but not actually "live" them. An easy indication of firm culture is whether attorneys lead and encourage a balanced life or whether the firm is a place where work must always come first. Similarly, whether the firm is formal or informal (as reflected in dress, salutations, titles, or status consciousness) reflects culture. Most law firms' business models are based on the billable hour and therefore productivity and profitability are often used as measures of success. Culture varies, however, in terms of the level of billable hours required (some as high as 2,200 per year, some as low as 1,400) and whether the firm sets aside a percentage of profits each year to invest in things like talent investments and capital improvements including technology or distributes all profits every year.

Accountability and compensation are two additional ways culture can be evaluated. For example, are leaders and managers provided job descriptions, asked to devise annual goals and then measured against and compensated accordingly? Other critical culture indicators are what is measured and rewarded at the partner and employee levels, how performance review and compensation processes are administered, whether they are perceived to be fair and transparent, and whether partners and employees are rewarded for individual achievement or team collaboration. Too often, firms state they have a "no jerks allowed" rule but don't actually penalize or remove partners and employees who have a negative or destructive effect on others in the firm – so bad behavior is tolerated despite a stated value to the contrary. For some firms, how involved lawyers and employees are in their external communities and whether these are encouraged and supported by the firm can be an important cultural distinction. Finally, a clear indicator of cultural values is how budgets are created and resources allocated.

Talent development and management

How a firm invests in its people is a critical component to ensuring a healthy culture in which employees are engaged and want to remain at the firm. A fundamental difference among firms is whether there is equal effort to support development and skills of professional managers and support staff as there is of lawyers. Given how quickly things are changing in the workplace and in order to offer ample opportunities for growth and development within the firm, access to robust online and live training resources for upskilling and reskilling, as well as options for certification or advanced degrees, will indicate how committed the firm is to retaining employees and partners.

There has been a renewed focus on racial and gender injustice and inequalities in law firms so a firm's active promotion, support, and advancement of a diverse workforce, programs the firm has put in place to address bias and opportunity inequity, and whether the firm's leadership reflects diversity, will all provide strong indicators of cultural values. With lateral hiring serving as the top growth strategy of most law firms, culture can erode depending upon how and how effectively a firm evaluates potential lateral hires to ensure that they will support and fit in with the firm's culture. Similarly, how effectively the firm executes succession management of leaders, client relationship partners, and all other talent reflects its approach to talent management.

Governance and leadership

At a broad level, how decision-making happens and whether the firm is considered autocratic/dictatorial or democratic/managed by consensus as well as whether governance is transparent, all reflect and affect the core culture of a firm. Similarly, how the firm is financially managed, whether highly conservative or risk-oriented, significantly impact or reflect culture.

Increasingly, leadership and management responsibilities are being dispersed among many more partners and professional managers. The culture of a firm will be reflected in how clearly roles and expectations throughout the firm are defined and evaluated and how leaders and managers are evaluated and compensated. How the firm is led and managed, how leaders are selected and groomed, trained and coached, measured and rewarded, all reflect the investment a firm makes in its leadership. In a related vein, culture is defined by the degree to which decisions are made and power resides in those who do not have formal leadership titles or roles.

Collaboration, trust, and respect

One of the most frequently touted aspects of firm culture is collegiality. When asked what makes their culture special, lawyers in many firms will say "we are very collegial". In reality, few firms have highly collaborative cultures since very often partners are more focused on their own practices and personal earnings. Collegial also has become a misnomer for firms in which decision-making is done by consensus and where partners don't want to feel critical of each other or be held accountable so, as a result, often lack strong, directed governance.

This aspect of a firm's true culture can be observed in a number of ways, including by whom, how, and when communication happens in the firm, within departments, across seniority and generational levels as well as in different offices and whether all are able and encouraged to voice concerns or suggestions. Does the firm encourage or discourage interaction among lawyers and staff? Partners and associates? How accessible are partners to each other and others?

Another indicator of collaboration and trust is how effectively partners work together to build and expand client relationships and whether lawyers and staff give and share credit for successful outcomes, new business, and new ideas. On a related note, are clients considered "firm" clients or do partners control their own client relationships and resist introducing other partners? Similarly, do partners and practice groups operate in silos or do they collaborate together on firm and client initiatives and matters?

Culture is also observed through the degree to which social interaction is encouraged both while at work and outside the firm and how the firm schedules and structures events, meetings, and communications to enhance collegiality. In some firms, the firm's leadership makes a concerted effort to get to know spouses and families of all lawyers and staff. Another indicator of trust and collegiality is whether and how the firm stays in touch with alumni or whether it shuns former employees, associates and partners, especially those who go to competitors.

Consciously (re)create and manage your culture to compete in the future

Many firms have cultures by default – they are a result of history and happenstance and are usually not planned or directed. Firms are more profitable and productive when talent and culture are aligned around a positive, respectful work environment. In order to have a culture your firm intentionally creates and lives by, the firm will have to analyze what it learned from the assessment process, determine where it is falling short in the culture it desires, and put effective programs, policies, structures, and leadership in place to ensure compliance and accountability.

Recent events like the pandemic and racial injustice movement have provided the impetus and opportunity for firm leaders to look at their culture and reset the tone with a focus on humanity, diversity, and equality. To recalibrate aspects of a firm's culture that are weak or have a negative impact on employees will require discipline, buy-in, and patience, since change will occur best in smaller steps that can be measured, modified, and then celebrated.

Modify your vision, mission, strategy and decision-making

- Identify and publicly honor the strengths of your existing culture; determine areas for improvement or change.
- Update the firm's strategy based on findings of the culture assessment and market research.
- Refine/finalize the firm's core values and, once complete, create the necessary framework of policies, programs, and protocols to measure, monitor, and ensure improvement and compliance to each value.
- Develop systematic methods to seek input from employees, clients, and the broader marketplace to consider when modifying strategy and culture.
- Publish the firm's values to all employees – make them visible on the firm's intranet and consider publishing externally on the website.
- Align and modify the governance and leadership model to ensure successful oversight of and compliance with culture and values.

Develop systems and processes to support articulated values and norms

- Define, articulate and make public within the firm its goals and approaches for hiring, retention, diversity, training, promotion, compensation, budgeting, accountability, and recognition.

- Address and improve the methods/modes and frequency of communication to ensure that all stakeholders feel apprised of firm policies, news, new initiatives and opportunities to be involved, and that there are systems in place to welcome two-way communication.
- Train leaders and managers in executing policies, monitoring behaviors, and addressing any noncompliant behaviors.
- Devise a system for retrieving ongoing feedback on how the firm and its leaders and employees are living the values and following norms, including a "safe place" for employees to lodge concerns or complaints.
- Involve senior professionals in helping to lead and manage culture initiatives at the strategic level and provide the authority to address any deficiencies.

Align talent, roles, and responsibilities with the firm's future needs

- Conduct a workforce gap analysis – work distribution, staffing models, skills requirements by role and level, contract/temp workers.
- Reskill, retool, and redeploy existing employees before hiring new employees.
- Hire and promote for diverse and collaborative teams; train interviewers.
- Build diversity, inclusion, and opportunity equity programs that can and are measured for outcomes.
- Match recruiting to firm strategy, practice/client needs, and new skill requirements.
- Use personality assessments for cultural fit/predictive success – lateral partners and lateral groups especially need to be screened for cultural fit.
- Build core competency models and customized development programs.
- Use promotion, advancement, compensation, and bonuses to reward for highest in-demand skills.
- Consider how to leverage skills of senior partners, professional managers, and staff past retirement age (but don't block advancement of younger talent).
- Don't segregate lawyers and "non-lawyers".

Refine and align the firm's brand with its culture

- Develop a strong value proposition for prospective employees/partners based on what current employees say drew them to the firm.
- Seek ongoing feedback internally and externally (from employees, recruits, clients, search firms, law schools, colleagues, and tech schools) to ensure that the brand being promoted resonates with the actual culture.
- Assess retention factors to determine what is making people leave the firm and what will make top talent stay.
- Include "cultural fit" and accountability measurements in performance reviews as well as ability and willingness to retool, upskill, and be flexible.
- Make sure employees can fully understand, appreciate, and live the firm's values.

Improve employee engagement by managing the work experience

- Measure levels of engagement of lawyers and staff with regular surveys and one-on-one conversations.
- Be transparent about career paths, work options, criteria, and advancement processes.
- Celebrate diversity, collaboration, and innovation.
- Establish intolerance and related penalties for behaviors that violate cultural values.
- Enable cross-functional, cross-role, cross-practice short-term projects.
- Provide real time feedback and mentoring.
- Provide world class training and on-demand learning.
- Make work meaningful.
- Address remote/virtual workforce conditions and challenges.

Monitor and manage your culture

- Identify areas that will reinforce or impede culture and continuously evaluate these.
- Establish goals and benchmarks to track progress and milestones.

- Use data to measure success or slippage, e.g. surveys to gauge employee engagement and exit interviews to evaluate attrition.
- Create safe "spaces" and methods for employees to regularly share issues or concerns that contrast with the firm's stated cultural norms and values.
- Include behaviors that comprise, contribute to, and define the firm's cultural values and norms as specific skills and characteristics built into performance reviews, advancement, and remuneration.
- Include culture and its component parts in every internal meeting agenda throughout the year (not just at an annual partners' retreat).
- Communicate and celebrate your successes and express appreciation.

Creating a healthy culture will make employees more productive, firms more profitable, and will provide a competitive advantage in the marketplace. Recent disruptions have put a lot of pressure on firm leaders to assess and address the human impacts that the pandemic and racial and gender inequities have had on all partners, associates, and staff, and to build the kind of approaches, systems, and protocols that support more caring and collaborative cultures. This will require immediate attention to assess and recalibrate the firm's current culture and ongoing oversight to ensure that policies and programs support core value, vision, and collective respect.

Chapter 6:
Promoting lawyer wellbeing – lessons learned from the ABA wellbeing pledge campaign

By Bree Buchanan, founding co-chair of the National Task Force on Lawyer Well-Being, and Jonathan Beitner, chair of the American Bar Association's Commission on Lawyers Assistance Programs' Well-Being Committee

Lawyer wellbeing movement launches pledge campaign

When the National Task Force on Lawyer Well-Being[1] published its groundbreaking report *The Path to Lawyer Well-Being: Practical Recommendations for Positive Change*[2] in 2017, its authors could never have predicted the cataclysmic changes in store for the legal profession – and the entire world – with the onset of the COVID-19 pandemic. Studies in the United States had already revealed an unsustainable rate of behavioral health issues among lawyers.[3] Now, in 2020, the unprecedented disruptions facing law firms are bringing on intensified concerns regarding heightened stress, anxiety, depression, and substance use issues.

Fortunately, the report outlines strategies for legal employers who are not only looking to shift their culture towards one that is more sustainable for their staff, but also for those seeking to address the expected wave of behavioral health issues that will likely follow in the wake of the pandemic.[4] In setting forth a foundational definition of "wellbeing", the report's authors adopted a broad and inclusive approach, one that addresses both the identification and treatment of behavioral health issues, as well as promotes thriving across multiple dimensions for all members of the profession.[5]

In particular, the report's recommendations for legal employers address a firm's organizational structure, employment policies and practices, programming and educational initiatives, the role of alcohol in firm events, the development of relationships with lawyer wellbeing experts, and the provision of confidential access to resources.[6] To promote the report's recommendations for legal employers and encourage their adoption, the American Bar Association (ABA) formed the Working Group to Advance Well-Being in the Legal Profession.[7]

The Working Group quickly launched the ABA's wellbeing pledge, a seven-point framework by which signatories commit to providing ongoing education regarding the mental health issues disproportionately affecting lawyers, "disrupting the status quo of drinking-based events", providing confidential access to resources, as well as developing policies and protocols to support the assessment and treatment of behavioral health conditions.[8] At the time of writing, 187 global firms, law schools, bar associations, government agencies, corporate legal departments, and other legal employers have signed the pledge.[9]

In the spring of 2020, signatories reported the progress they made towards fulfilling the pledge's terms during the past year. Their responses demonstrate that, with encouragement and guidance, legal employers are beginning to shift the culture towards one that better respects and supports the wellbeing of its members. This chapter summarizes those reports, giving legal professionals and those charged with steering their firm through our current uncharted waters insight into how systemic efforts to promote wellbeing can be achieved.[10] Given the role of wellbeing in enhancing productivity, job satisfaction, retention and risk management, savvy legal professionals will do well to consider adopting some of the strategies outlined below to promote not just surviving, but also thriving during these difficult times.

Pledge signatories' wellbeing initiatives

Embed wellbeing in organizational infrastructure

Understanding that systemic change is best institutionalized when a supportive infrastructure is adopted, the report's authors encourage firms to create a lawyer wellbeing committee or, at the least, to appoint a wellbeing advocate. This group or individual should be tasked with "evaluating the work environment, identifying and addressing policies and procedures that create the greatest mental distress among employees, identifying how best to promote a positive state of wellbeing, and tracking progress of wellbeing strategies".[11] While signatories were not specifically charged with modifying their organizational infrastructure, many found this to be a foundational approach to implementing the report's recommendations and complying with their pledge commitments.

Signatories reported housing their wellbeing efforts in a variety of organizational structures, and it is clear that there are many approaches firms can take. For example, some firms' wellbeing programs and policies are developed and implemented by their HR department, while others are the province of the talent management or professional development groups. Many firms followed the report's recommendation to create a wellbeing committee, while others designated specific wellbeing advocates or champions in each office. Still others combined these ideas and took a multi-department approach to promoting the health and wellness of their attorneys and staff. Finally, one trend that has emerged in recent years is the creation of full-time positions dedicated specifically to bolstering wellbeing at the firm. Several large, international firms now have directors or managers of wellbeing, with at least one firm having a chief wellbeing officer.

Despite the multitude of strategies for structuring who or what departments are responsible for overseeing wellness initiatives, there are several tenets that are universally applicable and critical for implementing successful wellbeing programs. First, it is essential to get buy-in from firm leadership and to establish well-respected and highly visible wellbeing champions. Some firms have found it beneficial to enlist office managing partners or other high-ranking lawyers to promote – or even put on – wellbeing programming. Others report success with having members of firm leadership share their struggles with maintaining their own wellbeing over the course of their career, and some even shared their experiences of recovering from mental health or substance use problems.

In addition to getting buy-in at the top, it is also important to cultivate a broad base of support by engaging associates and staff. Oftentimes, these groups are quite interested in taking advantage of wellbeing programs and resources but may feel discouraged if they do not have confidence that doing so would be supported by the partners they work with. This is another reason why it is so important to make sure firm leadership champions wellbeing initiatives.

An easy way to engage associates and staff is to create a wellbeing committee comprised of attorneys and staff of all levels and across all offices. Firms have also included associates and staff in the process for selecting wellbeing vendors, resources, and speakers. Another innovative way to encourage associates to participate in wellbeing initiatives is to provide billable hour credits for doing so – a tactic many firms have taken to promote pro bono work, business development, and other non-billable activities. For example, one international firm recently introduced a policy by which associates receive credit for up to 25 hours spent learning about or practicing mindfulness while offering several workshops and programs on the topic throughout the year.

Using internal surveys is another way to gauge interest, engagement, and the efficacy of wellbeing efforts among associates and staff. At least one global law firm has included questions related to mental health and substance use, as well as a discussion of the firm's commitment to the pledge, as part of its annual associate review process.

Finally, it is important to think about the ways in which a firm's wellbeing offerings and benefits are communicated to attorneys and staff. Most firms have dedicated spaces on their intranet websites where wellbeing programs and resources are advertised. Many firms have gone further and branded their wellness programs to help raise awareness and visibility. Some examples include Seyfarth & Shaw LLP's "SeyfarthLife", Latham & Watkins LLP's "LiveWell Latham", and Morgan Lewis LLP's "ML Well". These brands are also highlighted in external communications and as part of firms' recruiting efforts for law students and lateral hires. Another creative idea at least one firm implemented was creating a business-card sized overview of the firm's EAP and other wellbeing resources, as well as instructions on how to access them.

Regardless of how a law firm structures its wellbeing offerings, adhering to the principles discussed above will help ensure that the efforts and resources devoted to promoting wellbeing have the greatest impact.

Establish policies and practices to support wellbeing

Like creating an infrastructure that supports wellbeing, establishing policies and practices that directly address behavioral health impairments of staff are essential to bringing a shift in law firm culture. The report encourages employers to "establish a confidential reporting procedure for lawyers and staff to convey concerns about their colleagues' mental health or substance use internally," or for themselves without being penalized or stigmatized.[12] Written, proactive policies provide transparency and a sense of fairness regarding what to expect if one needs help or suspects the impairment of a colleague. Designating a person(s) to whom reports are made will promote consistency in how situations are addressed and will help reduce the fear and stigma surrounding seeking help.

The creators of the pledge, keenly aware of the powerful stigma of having a substance use or mental health disorder, included this recommendation from the report and specifically provided that policies should be both transparent and ensure confidentiality. The importance of maintaining mindfulness regarding the role of stigma can hardly be understated. The 2016 Lawyer Study that launched the lawyer wellbeing movement revealed that attorneys are highly avoidant of help-seeking or taking any actions that could indicate they might be experiencing a mental health or substance use problem. For example, only seven percent of attorneys identified as having "problematic drinking" habits[13] received services to treat the condition.[14] Likewise, a 2014 nationwide survey of American law students found that while 42 percent of respondents felt they had needed mental health assistance over the past year, only half of those students actually received help.[15] In both studies, respondents indicated that their reluctance to seek treatment was driven by fear that "someone would find out" about their struggles and that their ability to enter the profession, find a job, and excel would be adversely affected. Perhaps the most startling statistic regarding the pervasive nature of stigma around these issues came from the Law Student Survey, which found that 62 percent of law students believed seeking help for a mental health or substance use issue would negatively impact their job or academic standing.[16]

The working group that launched the pledge also created a "well-being template for legal employers" – essentially a guide for drafting a comprehensive HR policy that specifically addresses situations involving a substance use or mental health problem. The template includes a designation of to whom reports should be made, a declaration regarding the confidential nature of any investigations or actions taken, and a clear statement of expectations for both the firm and employees.[17] Shortly after implementing this policy and setting out a clear protocol for seeking treatment, one firm reported seeing multiple employees come forward to get help. Numerous signatories indicated they had used this template to update their policies, often to supplement existing leave and disability policies. Some signatories reported having a "ramp up" program to allow those returning from getting treatment to slowly build back up to standard billable requirements. One large firm reported offering a "return to work mentor".

De-emphasizing the expectation of alcohol

In response to data showing significantly elevated rates of problem drinking in the legal profession, the report contains a general recommendation for all stakeholders to limit alcohol consumption.[18] Specifically, it encourages stakeholders to "de-emphasize the expectation of alcohol" and to "plan social events that provide a variety of alternative non-alcoholic beverages and [to] consider other types of activities to promote socializing and networking". Overall, social norms should be developed "which both discourage heavy drinking and encourage those in need to seek help for problem use".[19]

Reasons to institute changes regarding the role of alcohol in law firm culture are numerous. Traditionally, drinking alcohol has been the way most losses are grieved and successes are celebrated, with alcohol's presence being a central focus at firm gatherings. This over-emphasis can create a culture in which lawyers and law students come to believe that they must imbibe alcohol to be a part of the law firm team. This social climate makes it exceedingly difficult for those with a tendency towards problem drinking and further stigmatizes those seeking help or in recovery. It also has the effect of excluding lawyers who do not drink – due to religious or other personal reasons – from these essential networking and team-building events, thereby thwarting firm efforts to promote inclusivity.[20] Additionally, unacceptable behaviors such as sexual harassment or assault tend to occur when alcohol flows freely, creating additional risk management concerns for firms.

Pledge signatories demonstrated an impressive array of creative ways in which to "de-emphasize" alcohol in their firm's culture. Broadly speaking, these efforts tended to fall into one of three categories: (1) structuring more creative events beyond "happy hours", (2) making non-alcoholic options more attractive, and (3) implementing policies explicitly aimed at reducing alcohol consumption.

By far the most common strategy for reducing the expectation of alcohol at events was to diversify when and where events were held – with a conscious effort to limit "happy hour" events. Many firms reported holding breakfast and lunch meetings and events more often, or changing previously advertised "happy hours" to "social hours". Another common approach was to hold more activity-based events. Instead of having appetizers and cocktails at a bar, firms were partaking in cooking classes, trivia nights, bowling, book clubs, and axe-throwing. Many firms have also increased their number of community- or service-based activities, such as volunteering at food banks, building homes with Habitat for Humanity, or partnering with a local charity. By de-emphasizing alcohol and holding events outside of the happy hour time slot, firms have been able to host more family-friendly events, allowing parents and other caretakers to participate while also providing a different way of fostering social connections and collegiality among attorneys and staff.

In addition to rethinking where and when events are held, firms also reported making a conscious effort to make non-alcoholic options more attractive. Having events that are focused on food – such as taco stands, ice cream socials, smoothie or juice bars, and gourmet coffee options – is another way to break the traditional "happy hour" paradigm while also highlighting non-alcoholic offerings. During events where alcohol is served many firms also provided specialty mocktails, with several creating signature mocktails named after the firm or a managing partner.

Firms also implemented new policies aimed at reducing alcohol consumption at events. For example, several firms reduced the hours during which alcohol is served, enacted cash bars, limited consumption with the use of drink tickets, or stopped serving hard liquor. Others have banned the practice of throwing firm-sponsored after-parties or reduced their budgets for alcohol at social events. One pledge signatory assigned the HR professional in charge of event planning to its well-being committee in order to ensure events reflected and promoted their wellness goals and priorities. Another now has a policy of no longer holding events around alcohol-focused activities, such as wine tastings and brewery tours. To get a better sense of their office's culture around these issues, some signatories conducted internal surveys to see if attorneys and staff felt pressure to drink at events.

Finally, several firms referenced the importance of providing additional information and programming around alcohol use and how to reach out for help if you think you or a friend, colleague, or family member is misusing alcohol or other substances. Often, these resources directed employees to the firm's EAP or that office's local Lawyers Assistance Program. Some signatories have also teamed up with entities like Alcohol Change for guidance on how to reduce alcohol consumption and risky drinking behaviors and attitudes.[21]

Wellbeing programming and educational initiatives

Recommendation 26 of the report encourages all legal employers to "provide education and training on wellbeing-related topics and recruit experts to help them do so".[22] The authors specifically point out that orientation and onboarding programs should incorporate wellbeing subject matter. Introducing this topic from the first day signals "its importance to the organization and will start the process of developing skills that may help prevent wellbeing problems".[23] The report also contains an extensive list of educational topics in Appendix B.[24]

The pledge builds from this recommendation by requiring signatories to provide educational opportunities on topics related to mental health, substance use, and wellbeing.[25] Common topics that firms reported providing programming around include building resilience, practicing mindfulness, fostering more positivity/optimism, financial wellbeing, nutrition, and understanding the signs and symptoms of mental health and substance use, as well as how to handle a suicidal situation. More and more, these programs are being embedded into new attorney orientations, summer associate training, and professional development curricula.

Whether through educational programming, e-newsletters, websites, or online resource hubs, firms should also make sure that all staff are aware of resources available through the firm (such as behavioral health insurance; EAPs) or external sources (lawyers assistance programs)[26] that can assist in the event of a mental health or substance use issue. To that end, one prong of the pledge encourages signatories to provide free and confidential self-assessment tools regarding mental health and substance use issues.[27] Emphasizing the confidential nature of these resources will promote utilization and help diminish fears stemming from seeking help.

As part of the recommendation to provide educational programming, legal employers are encouraged to partner with wellbeing subject matter experts. In particular, lawyer assistance programs are singled out as a particularly rich source of expertise when dealing with not only the intervention and treatment of behavioral health problems, but also general topics related to wellbeing. The report recommends "state-based lawyer assistance programs [as] indispensable partners in efforts to educate and empower the legal profession to identify, treat, and prevent conditions at the root of the current wellbeing crisis, and to create lawyer-specific programs and access to treatment".[28] This recommendation mirrors another component of the pledge, which requires signatories to develop visible partnerships with outside wellbeing experts – including local LAPs.[29]

While the majority of signatories collaborated with their local LAP and offered robust benefits packages through an EAP, several firms also worked with other outside entities that focus on mental health and substance use issues. For example, firms reported partnering with organizations such as NAMI, the American Counseling Association, Mental Health America, the JED Foundation, the National Council of Behavioral Health, the Hazelden-Betty Ford Foundation, the British Heart Foundation, and Alcohol Change. Others organized programs and resources in conjunction with health care providers like the Mayo Clinic, Blue Cross Blue Shield, and the Cleveland Clinic.

Several firms also brought in outside trainers to offer mental health first aid certification programs[30] to their attorneys and staff. Many firms offered these trainings to firm leaders and members of the HR department, as those individuals may be more likely to encounter or be in a position to assist an employee dealing with a mental health or substance use issue.

A word of caution and a call to action

The ABA wellbeing pledge campaign challenged legal employers to join the growing lawyer wellbeing movement that is spreading across the globe. By providing firms with ideas for initiatives and goals to work towards, the pledge has leaned into the inherently competitive nature of the legal industry. In response, signatories are enthusiastically and creatively developing strategies so the legal profession can foster, rather than impede, the wellbeing of its members. Given the unprecedented test of adaptability and resilience presented by the COVID-19 pandemic, these strategies are needed now more than ever.

In closing, a common challenge noted by many signatories deserves attention. Those in charge of wellbeing initiatives repeatedly lamented the difficulty in getting lawyers, staff, and firm management to pay attention to them. One signatory aptly observed that balancing a commitment to wellbeing with the commitment to excellent client service was "a constant challenge". This perceived competition between taking time for self-care and putting in time towards billable hours lies at the crux of the lawyer wellbeing movement.

To successfully bring about change in how the legal profession addresses the wellbeing of its members, HR professionals and firm leadership must come to understand "[t]he benefits of increased lawyer wellbeing are compelling and the cost of lawyer impairment are too great to ignore". Rather than taking a hands-off approach to these issues and "only dealing with them when forced to because of impairment that can no longer be ignored", legal employers must do more to help lawyers be, get, and stay well.[31] To quote the closing words of the report:

> *"As a profession, we have the capacity to face these challenges and create a better future for our lawyers that is sustainable. We can do so – not in spite of – but in pursuit of the highest professional standards, business practices, and ethical ideals."*[32]

References

1. The National Task Force on Lawyer Well-Being is leading a culture shift in law to establish health and wellbeing as core centerpieces of professional success. See https://lawyerwellbeing.net.
2. The National Task Force on Lawyer Well-Being (2017). *The Path to Lawyer Well-Being: Practical Recommendations for Positive Change*. https://lawyerwellbeing.net/wp-content/uploads/2017/11/Lawyer-Wellbeing-Report.pdf.
3. An ABA and Hazelden Betty Ford Foundation study published in 2016 of nearly 13,000 currently-practicing lawyers found that between 21 and 36

percent qualify as problem drinkers, and that approximately 28 percent, 19 percent, and 23 percent are struggling with some level of depression, anxiety, and stress, respectively. Notably, this study found that younger lawyers in the first ten years of practice and those working in private firms experience the highest rates of problem drinking and depression. It also highlighted the extreme reluctance of those suffering to access any sort of assistance or treatment, primarily due to stigma, shame, and fear of being "found out". P. R. Krill, R. Johnson, & L. Albert, "The Prevalence of Substance Use and Other Mental Health Concerns Among American Attorneys", 10 *J. Addiction Med.* 46 (2016). To access this study: https://journals.lww.com/journaladdictionmedicine/Fulltext/2016/02000/The_Prevalence_of_Substance_ Use_and_Other_Mental.8.aspx.

4. Krill, Patrick (30 June 2020). *The Events of 2020 Have Changed Our Collective Mental Health – and Risk – Profile*. Law.Com. www.law.com/2020/06/30/the-events-of-2020-have-changed-our-collective-mental-health-and-risk-profile/; see also Cohen, Arienne (20 April 2020) *A second silent pandemic could sweep the country alongside COVID-19.* Fast Company. https://www.fastcompany.com/90492874/a-second-silent-pandemic-will-sweep-the-country-alongside-covid-19.
5. The National Task Force's Report defines lawyer wellbeing as "a continuous process whereby lawyers seek to thrive in each of the following areas: emotional health, occupational pursuits, creative or intellectual endeavors, sense of spirituality or greater purpose in life, physical health, and social connections with others." National Task Force, *Path to WellBeing*, 9.
6. The report directed recommendations to all stakeholder groups that comprise the legal profession: the judiciary, regulators, legal employers, law schools, malpractice carriers, and lawyers assistance programs. General recommendations directed to all stakeholders were also set out in the report.
7. Beyond the authors of the report, thanks are also due to those who made the pledge campaign possible, including Patrick Krill who developed the tenets of the pledge, former ABA presidents Hilarie Bass and Bob Carlson who created and supported the working group, staff of the ABA Commission on Lawyers Assistance Program (CoLAP) who manage the pledge campaign, as well as members of the CoLAP Committee who administer it.
8. A slide deck outlining the pledge can be found at: www.americanbar.org/content/dam/aba/administrative/lawyer_assistance/ls_colap_working_group_pledge_and_campaign.PDF.
9. An updated list of signatories can be found at: https://www.americanbar.org/groups/lawyer_assistance/resources/lap_programs_by_state/.
10. Many initiatives discussed below are based upon pledge signatory reports of their actions taken during the 2019-2020 bar year. Due to representations made as to the confidentiality of these reports, firm and employer names are not included. In instances where a firm is explicitly mentioned by name, the authors obtained permission to release the information contained in this chapter or it was obtained from a publicly available source, such as press releases or a firm's website.

11. National Task Force, *Path to WellBeing*, 31.
12. Ibid. 32.
13. "Problematic use" of alcohol, or "problematic drinking" is defined as use that is "hazardous or harmful," as well as "use that warrants a full diagnostic evaluation for alcohol use disorder." Krill. *Prevalence of Substance Abuse*, 47.
14. *Ibid.* 50.
15. Jerome M. Organ, David B. Jaffe & Katherine M. Bender, Ph.D., "Suffering in Silence: The Survey of Law Student Well-Being and the Reluctance of Law Students to Seek Help for Substance Use and Mental Health Concerns", 66 *J. Legal Educ.* 116 (Autumn 2016).
16. Ibid. 140.
17. The template can be found at: www.americanbar.org/content/dam/aba/administrative/lawyer_assistance/well-being-template-for-legal-employers-final-3-19.pdf.
18. National Task Force, *Path to WellBeing*, 19.
19. *Ibid.*
20. Staff members may avoid alcohol for a variety of reasons, including personal preference. They may practice a religion or have a medical condition that prevents their use of alcohol. They may be responsible for small children or elders.
21. *See* https://alcoholchange.org.uk.
22. National Task Force, *Path to WellBeing*, 33.
23. *Ibid.*
24. *Ibid.*, 50-57.
25. See note 10, supra.
26. To find a directory of Lawyers Assistance Programs, go to: www.americanbar.org/groups/lawyer_assistance/resources/lap_programs_by_state/.
27. See note 10, supra.
28. National Task Force, *Path to Well-Being*, 14.
29. See note 10, supra.
30. To learn more about Mental Health First Aid, see: www.mentalhealthfirstaid.org/.
31. National Task Force, *Path to WellBeing*, 10.
32. *Ibid.*, 47.

Chapter 7:

Resilience and wellbeing for the legal profession during the time of COVID-19 and beyond

By Renee Branson, MA, CReC, principal founder, RB Consulting

The intense heat of a kiln is a crisis point in which one of two things will happen: weaknesses in the clay will be exposed and the object will shatter, or the clay will hold, allowing the particles to weld together into a stronger and more beautiful ceramic. Lowly mud combined with fire is a test that results in destruction or creation of something new. COVID-19 is the kiln that is testing our communities, families, and economy. The disruption and trauma caused by the COVID-19 pandemic crisis is indisputable. It is hard to name one industry, community, or individual not impacted. Coronavirus has created vulnerabilities to our physical, financial, and mental health. Vulnerabilities, however painful, often serve to shine a light on what has long needed to be repaired, dismantled, or innovated. Lawyers, and others in the profession, may not often openly talk about stress, burnout, mental illness, and substance abuse, but they have always been there in the shadows. Now, with the added weight of a pandemic, the bright side is that it has given us the opportunity to talk more freely about our mental wellbeing than we have before. For the legal profession, this can be one silver lining in a very dark cloud. It can provide the opportunity to become more resilient in the face of crisis, challenge, and change.

It is important to first understand how we define these concepts of disruption, resilience, and wellbeing. Disrupt has two definitions: "to interrupt by causing a disturbance or problem", or "to drastically destroy the structure of something". The pandemic is an interruption at best and destruction at worst. How we adapt to it and learn from it has the ability to increase our wellbeing and resilience long after the current crisis. Wellbeing is composed of three primary pillars – autonomy (being in control of your own life), self-efficacy (being competent and capable to succeed and thrive), and purpose (finding meaning in one's lived experience). If wellbeing is the "what" we are trying to achieve, resilience is the "how". Resilience is a set of skills and traits that work together to increase our wellbeing.

Whether the disruption being faced is one of mere interruption or total destruction, it impedes a person's ability to function in the same way they previously had. Disruption wrecks our homeostasis. Our brains come to a screeching halt to assess what to do next and how to get it done. This is particularly challenging for lawyers because the tools most commonly relied upon in the profession – such as critical thinking and problem solving – are literally harder to access when we are in crisis. When stress impacts the brain, cognitive functioning, motivation, creativity, grit, and collaboration can be stunted. Two hundred thousand years of human biology has trained the brain to focus its activity on surviving, not thriving, when it believes it is under attack. The brain triggers a physical response resulting in an elevated heart rate, increased blood pressure, tense muscles, and shortness of breath. This less resilient mind will take the stimulus created by the disruption and allow the amygdala or "lizard brain" to take over – fight, flight, or freeze. Essentially, the "lizard brain" prepares the physical body for impact and robs the "thinking brain" of its ability to be creative and solution focused. What this looks like on the outside is a person who is resistant to change. One person might shut down and refuse to engage in collaboration. Another might argue and "rage against the dying of the light" about the way things used to be. Yet another might simply not be able or willing to understand the inevitability of change. At worst, people experience anxiety, depression, or other mental health challenges that can result in poor coping mechanisms.

A resilient mind will form new synapses and pathways to address the new information. It allows the mind to be self-nurturing, adaptable, and innovative. What this looks like on the outside is a person who is able to maintain composure in the midst of disruption, respond with reason, approach with grit, and rely on collaboration to address the changing environment. Every person has a natural capacity for resilience. Much like other personality traits, varying levels of resilience are "baked in" us from the beginning depending on our unique personality, our experiences, and our environments. That is not to say resilience is static, however. Resilience can be cultivated and developed. Like a muscle, it can strengthen or atrophy depending on how we exercise it.

How, then, do people cultivate this skill? First is by understanding what makes up resilience. There are six different domains that make up human resilience – connection, calm, health, reasoning, optimism, and integrity. Generally speaking, lawyers and other legal professionals have a tendency to be stronger in some of these areas and need growth in others. The different domains of resilience can be thought of as books in a library. Some are well used and committed to memory while others require us to pull them off the shelf to sharpen our knowledge. Similarly, depending on the circumstance, some resilience skills are more helpful in meeting the immediate need. We can hone and use what we need from the library, as long as we actually know what books are on the shelf.

Connection

Our need for connection is hardwired in each of us from the time of birth. We need it in our personal lives and we need it in our professional lives. It is in the realm of a lawyer's professional life that this can sometimes be a challenge. Again, speaking in general terms, the legal profession is a lonely one. People within a firm tend to work in silos where collaboration is often undervalued. Combined with naturally solitary work, the culture of perfectionism, fear of failure, and stigma around looking "weak" disconnects us from our colleagues. It requires people to be less authentic and, therefore, less "seen". How does this impact wellbeing? Legal professionals often describe the work pace as exhausting and it absolutely *is* exhausting. However, studies show us that when we feel alone in the face of crisis, challenge, or change, we experience the mental and physical fatigue much more acutely. Many hands make for light work in our emotional lives as well as our professional lives.

Skill builder

Take a sticky note and fold it in quarters so you have a small square. On one side, make a list of those in your personal and professional life with whom you can be fully authentic. These are who you can go to when you feel overwhelmed or frustrated. They are the ones whose opinions and help you trust. The size of your square is small for a reason. It only takes meaningful connection with a few people to have a dramatic impact on your wellbeing.

Calm

The ability to calm and self-soothe is one of our earliest skills. The more we were nurtured with deep connection early on, the easier we learned to self-soothe. In babies and young children this looks like sucking on a pacifier and cuddling with a special blanket or stuffed animal. As we age, however, those calming techniques are not socially acceptable.

We learn to calm and self-soothe in other ways. Some of those ways are healthy, while others are maladaptive. It can be easy for people to mistake numbing discomfort for calming discomfort. This is a primary cause of substance abuse or other addictive behavior like shopping, sex, gambling, or internet use. The problem (aside from the more obvious physical problems with some of these coping mechanisms) is that we cannot selectively numb mental and emotional discomfort. When we numb stress, sadness, or loneliness with a bottle of wine or hours on the internet, we are also numbing joy, peace, and true connection. The ability to calm ourselves and not numb requires us to feel the emotion we are experiencing (being present in the moment), while not allowing it to knock us off our feet (staying grounded and centered). This can be done through mindfulness, meditation, and simple yet intentional breathing technique. These skills encourage us to slow down – slow our breathing, slow our heart rate, and even slow our pace. For many lawyers, "slow" is not in their vocabulary. Slow feels undisciplined, lazy, or inefficient. In truth, however, moments of calm actually improve our cognitive functioning and productivity.

Skill builder

Try triangle breathing. Triangle breathing is simple to learn and can be practiced alone or in the middle of a meeting, if necessary. It is completely invisible to anyone else. The steps are this:

1. Inhale for a count of four.
2. Hold for a count of four.
3. Exhale for a count of eight.

Exhaling triggers our parasympathetic system, which slows our heart rate and our breathing while allowing tense muscles to ease. By simply extending the exhale, we experience calm.

Optimism

Lawyers have a tendency toward skepticism, cynicism, and pessimism because those are traits that are rewarded in the legal profession. It is what makes a lawyer good at the job. She is able to see the flaw in the contract that could cost a client millions. He can discern when a witness is not being forthcoming. These are useful tools. These tools, when applied incorrectly or to the wrong context, can lead to poor wellbeing.

When our larger worldview is only through the lens of skepticism, much remains out of focus. Still, it can be difficult to feel optimistic when we are overburdened and dealing with grim realities. To that, it is imperative to remember that optimism is not cheerfulness, rose-colored glasses, or unchecked naiveté. Grounded optimism takes reality into account while believing that challenges can be met with grit, gratitude, and grace.

Skill builder

Remember the three Ps of optimism. Optimism is the belief that the current crisis, challenge, or change is not:

- Permanent – it will not last forever.
- Pervasive – there are things not negatively impacted.
- Personal – it is not happening because of you or solely to you.

Reason

Reason is often the strongest resilience skill for those in the legal profession. Reason is the ability to anticipate and plan, be adaptable, and recognize opportunity. When our reasoning ability is honed, we are able to use stress as an opportunity to grow and reach goals that were previously unattainable. In order to do this, we need to be able to maintain our cognitive functioning and think through the stress. This requires us to regain composure (see "Calm"), ask for help, expand our knowledge, and be willing to take risks.

Skill builder

What kind of thinker are you? Knowing what kind of thinker you are will help you identify your reasoning strengths during crisis, challenge, or change.

- The *intuitive thinker* leaps from one idea to the next. The intuitive thinker is good at quick problem solving. This type of thinking is helpful when the problem requires and values speed over accuracy.
- The *systemic thinker* plans each move step by step. The systemic thinker is very thorough in problem solving and is forward thinking. This is helpful when accuracy of the solution is more important than the speed of the solution.

Integrity

Our values and integrity are put to the test when we are experiencing crisis, challenge, or change. This is true for our individual integrity and organizational integrity. For purposes of understanding how it relates to resilience, integrity is defined as congruence between our stated intrinsic values and our external behaviors. When we live outside of our own integrity, it has a caustic impact on our wellbeing. It creates added stress and strain to an already demanding situation. Unfortunately, during times of disruption and crisis, there is strong temptation to do what is quick or easy instead of courageously choosing what is right.

Skill builder

In moments of crisis, challenge, and change ask the following:

1. What value is most important to uphold right now?
2. Are my behaviors, decisions, and actions reflecting the values I am professing?
3. If not, what needs to change or be put in order for those to be congruent?

Health

Our bodies are our truth tellers. How we support our physical health impacts our mental health and vice versa. Listen to your body for signs of emotional distress. Depression and anxiety can manifest as chronic headaches, insomnia, gastrointestinal problems, high blood pressure and more. Even mild stress can be felt through a tightening of the muscles, sweating palms, rapid heart rate, and shallow breathing. These are signs to return to calming and self-soothing techniques. Conversely, how we treat our bodies can proactively combat stress and strain. Proper rest (which includes both sleep and mental relaxation) not only helps us manage stress, but also increases our cognitive functioning so we are better at finding solutions and being adaptive. Moderate exercise (just 20 minutes, four times a week) has been shown to ease symptoms of anxiety and depression. Foods that are high in calcium (yogurts and cheese), Omega-3 fats (salmon), and magnesium (dark, leafy greens) lowers cortisol (the stress hormone) and eases muscle tension.

Skill builder

When you are feeling particularly stressed, overwhelmed, or burned out, take notice of the following things such as:

- How much sleep and rest did you get the day before?
- Did you eat breakfast?
- When was the last time you took a walk, exercised, or simply spent time outside?

Noticing patterns in our behavioral health can point us to signs where we need to improve and care for ourselves.

We live in a time of unprecedented disruption in a profession that is notoriously full of stress and strain. When we proactively increase our resilience as a means of improving our mental wellbeing, not only do we bounce forward from crisis, challenge, and change, but we are better prepared for a healthier, happier life going forward.

Resilience – from personal practice to organizational priority

Individual professionals can implement these resilience skills into their lives and they will experience improved wellbeing. Until these skills become an organizational priority, however, the overall culture toward mental wellness will be slow to improve. Poor mental wellness in the legal profession has significant economic and performance impact. How, then, do firm leaders begin to prioritize resilience and wellbeing? Law firm leaders are familiar with the PPP of profits per partner; but there are another three Ps for leaders to consider when it comes to addressing wellbeing – personal, programming, and policy.

Personal

Law firm leaders must model the resilience skills they want to see in their stakeholders. They will understand that psychological safety is the number one indicator of high performance within teams and work toward cultivating the trust that allows for it. They will endeavor to see professionals within the firm in more holistic, human ways. They know that authentic relationships enhance not only resilience, but also commitment and engagement to the work. Sociology research professor, Brene Brown, states, "Leaders must either invest a reasonable amount of time attending to fears and feelings, or squander an unreasonable amount of time trying to manage ineffective and unproductive behavior".

Programming

Organizations invest in what they value. Law firm leaders who value the wellbeing of their professionals will invest in initiatives, training, and opportunities to support and strengthen emotional and mental wellness.

This can include enhanced mental health benefits, access to coaching (live or via an app), commitment to the ABA Well-Being Pledge, and ongoing professional development opportunities that focus on wellbeing.

Policy

Sound policy is a preventative measure against toxic work cultures and behaviors. Firm leaders committed to wellbeing will investigate whether existing policies incentivize the wrong behavior and course correct where needed. Do firms have "no a**hole" rules, but continue to compensate bad behavior by rainmakers? Do diversity and inclusion policies address the unique wellbeing needs of those who experience gender, racial, or other disparity? Are benefits such as sick leave, flexible work schedules, or continued remote work opportunities created to prioritize wellbeing? These are not simply altruistic needs to address; they have direct implications on the quality of work and reputation of a law firm.

Returning to the kiln, much before the pandemic, the legal industry was confronting the reality that mental wellbeing (or lack thereof) is a weakness in its clay. In a literal kiln, once the clay is put in the oven it's reached the point of no return; there is no fixing a flaw. Fortunately, law firm leaders can address these weaknesses, cultivate resilience, and strengthen wellbeing even in the midst of a crisis like COVID-19.

Chapter 8: Gen Z in COVID's cross-hairs – conversations to strengthen multi-generational teams

By Lauren Stiller Rikleen, president, Rikleen Institute for Strategic Leadership

Over the past decade, there has been a growing body of research and media coverage addressing generational challenges in the workplace, including differences in communication styles, work–life integration goals, expectations for advancement, and clarity in work assignments. In the legal profession, the level of uneasiness between partners and associates can be higher than in other workplace settings where there is a greater programmatic focus on talent retention and management.

These challenges have significant business development implications, both for law firms as a whole and for younger generations analyzing their own future opportunities within them. Accordingly, there is a need for the profession to address generational concerns holistically to ensure that the skills needed to build a client base are integrated into associate development.

Expanding the generational lens

Since Millennials began to enter the workforce in large numbers, most research addressing generational challenges focused on the need for Baby Boomers and Gen X to better understand, train, and support Millennials. Even when the advice offered was sound, however, senior generations bristled at the perceived expectation that they should shoulder the burden of strengthening multi-generational relationships. Too often, this perception only furthered tensions.

Although the conversations about Millennials – the older of whom are now well into their 30s – continue, the generational challenges must be seen through a much larger lens, as the post-Millennial generation moves through college, law school, and into the profession. This generation, the (poorly-named) Gen Z, includes the youngest members of the workforce, as well as those currently in secondary school or college.

Today, that larger lens is filled by the dominating event of 2020 – the global COVID-19 pandemic. Even as no one is spared its impacts, the direct and collateral damage will have life-altering effects on a young generation experiencing the pandemic during crucially formative years.

Lawyers should begin now to better understand and respond to post-COVID-19 workplace challenges. Part of that planning is the need to recognize that, even as each generation will be affected, some will have a stronger foundation from which to continue their career – and business – development skills while others will need greater support. The generational conversations must acknowledge what coronavirus has caused.

The first required step in the rebuilding process is to open lines of communication. In the absence of actual knowledge about each other, people fill gaps with inferred judgments that are infused by unconscious biases. The result can be heightened resentments and further misunderstanding.

When it comes to generational stereotypes, unconscious biases too often drive the conversation. Ask young professionals in the workplace what they know about the Boomers and Gen Xers with whom they work each day, and their lack of knowledge will likely reinforce the larger divide regarding how the generations perceive each other. Yet in order to move forward, it is helpful to first look back at how each of the generations got here.

Seeing Baby Boomers as they see themselves

Senior generations may openly express frustration with young people, but they do not fare well when those younger generations peer back up at them. Millennials, for example, may be close to their Boomer parents, have admired their Boomer teachers, and appreciated other older adults who helped them along the way, but Millennials' overall assessment of that generation's contributions to the workplace is more negative.

In the legal profession, the disapproval can be even worse. Young lawyers are confounded by a workplace where technology remains a tether, but not a tool. They cannot understand how commitment is still judged by physical presence as well as long hours, when technology offers and clients demand greater efficiencies. And they remain mystified by a hierarchical system marked by one road to success that often relegates those who choose a different path to stigma and diminished opportunities.

It is a harsh assessment that keeps younger lawyers wondering why workplaces are filled with written and unwritten rules that feel so intractable and partners who are too inaccessible. They see it as a dynamic that can and should be changed. But they also miss the history that is foundational to the behaviors.

It used to be that Baby Boomers got all the attention. They were the largest generation in history, and their adolescent years offered a range of extraordinary challenges during a time of enormous upheaval – civil rights demonstrations, Vietnam War protests, the second wave of the women's movement, as well as the assassination of a president, senator, and civil rights leader. At the same time, Boomers were leading a pop culture revolution, including the emergence of rock and roll, the rise of Motown, the dominance of the Beatles, and the excitement of Woodstock.

The list could go on but the point is clear. Boomers dominated a cultural moment whose impact continues to be felt. Yet when Boomer lawyers entered a workplace created by generations before them, they fit right in, generally following the model of the one-earner household where men served their clients and built their firms while their spouses took care of their families and home.

It proved to be an economic model that served a generation who applied its drive and energy from adolescence to career success. The psychic toll of that model, on the other hand, was often buried in a silence that preserved the status quo.

Gen X in the shadows

Boomers were followed by Generation X, a cohort tagged with a non-descript name that, because of its relatively small size, never achieved anywhere near the same level of attention as its predecessor and successor generations.

Their early years were marked by multiple recessions that fractured a long-standing bond of loyalty between corporations and their employees. They witnessed their families and neighbors coping with lay-offs that echoed in response to each economic downturn, resulting in workplace cultures in which job insecurity became a way of doing business.

The parents of Gen X had the highest divorce rate in history. The image of their fractured family lives resulted in a popular media refrain depicting Gen X "latch-key children" going to school with a key tied around their neck and coming home to watch MTV in an empty house until their parents returned from whatever jobs they could find.

The dramatic social transformations that rocked the early years of Boomers were not part of the Gen X experience. The fall of the Berlin Wall and the illegal sale of arms to Iran in order to fund the Nicaraguan Contras were major events of note, for those paying attention.

Ultimately, Xers emerged with a generational profile as a somewhat skeptical generation that wondered when their own time to shine would finally arrive. Too small to make big changes, they followed Boomers into the workplace and assimilated well, fitting into the rigid structure that had existed for decades.

Millennials – growing up optimistic in a scary world

Then came Millennials who, like the Boomers, were a large generation that garnered intense media scrutiny. But the generational profile that focused on the hyper-attentive and influential roles of parents, teachers, and coaches breezily misconstrued the importance and impact of these relationships.

In reality, having people in their lives who paid close attention may have been the saving grace for a generation whose early days of turmoil came in the form of domestic terrorism, gun violence in schools, and a growing opioid problem that moved from cities into smaller suburban and rural enclaves. The horrors of 9/11 and the global economic crisis that began in 2007 were calamitous events felt worldwide but, similar to COVID's impact on Gen Z, were traumatic life-altering events for Millennials emerging into adolescence and adulthood. Reality TV became their escape, along with a celebrity culture that oversold happiness in the form of seemingly never-ending consumer choice and social media "likes".

Many Millennials entering the legal profession when the economy collapsed were informed that their offers were rescinded, while others saw full-time opportunities become part-time jobs without benefits or, as new hires, became the first to be fired. A generation with an undeserved reputation for disloyalty had few options other than to change jobs frequently simply to keep up with rent payments and crushing law school debt.

Since their early years, Millennials have faced analysis, criticism, and dismissal which grew into a cacophony as they entered the workplace in increasing numbers. Through it all, the generation has persevered through societal turmoil, job changes, and downsizing, while survey data often shows them as nonetheless an optimistic cohort.

These shared experiences at a particularly vulnerable time in their lives contributed to a profile of a generation that is more likely to seek order in their world, transparency from their employers, and meaning in their work. Because of the small size of Gen X and the growing numbers of Boomer retirements, Millennials will also be needed to step into leadership roles at a younger age.

Gen Z interrupted

To those in law firms, members of Generation Z are currently in law school and younger. Critically, they will forever be the cohort who, in an instant, lost the important life-cycle milestones that also serve to build social and emotional development at important ages. Overnight, Gen Zers lost their daily interactions with the teachers who trained them, coaches who mentored them, clubs that fulfilled them, and friends who sustained them through the painful ordeals of youth. Key milestones of adolescence – proms, plays, athletics, and the ritual of graduation – vanished.

The implications are staggering. With interruptions in learning, travel, study abroad experiences, internships, volunteer opportunities, and other creative endeavors thwarted by social distancing requirements and travel restrictions, there will likely be a need to help this generation with skills development, stress management, and the building of emotional intelligence.

Building bridges

As each generation better understands the others, it will be easier to strengthen the teamwork that is essential to law firm success in the future.

What do Boomers wish younger generations understood about them? One place to start is by recognizing their activist roots. Many Boomers resist the perception that they are collectively responsible for climate change, fractured politics, institutional racism, illogically inflexible workplaces, and other seemingly endless examples of older workers choosing profits over families, health care, and individual protections.

Boomers want Millennials to understand their generation's role in the social upheaval and cultural transformation of the 1960s and early 1970s that informed their coming-of-age story and remain part of the values that many Boomers share today.

And how would Gen Xers like to be seen? First, they might want others to understand why they have not been significant change agents, and what it felt like to grow up and remain in the Boomers' overwhelming shadow, unable to create their own footprint.

Gen X's acquiescence to the workplace model likely emerged from their own insecurities in the profession. Having already endured multiple recessions and their parents' lay-offs, Xers were not inclined to take risks by advocating for workplace change opposed by resistant Boomers. Assimilation and hard work provided a degree of security that may have been missing previously.

Both Boomers and Xers found success in a difficult profession by building on a foundation that has endured through the years – work long hours, offer excellent client service, demonstrate loyalty by refusing to complain, and show a willingness to do more, even if family needs are sometimes sacrificed. This approach became part of their core identity, reinforced by a positive feedback loop rewarded by clients.

Factors that thwart change

Challenges to this entrenched way of working feel illogical when the results have been successful. Moreover, another dynamic is at work here. When generations of people have achieved success through personal sacrifice, one's unconscious biases offer a built-in resistance to change. Success on someone else's terms may feel like a direct challenge to a career of achievements.

After all, if I had to give up so much to get here, the thinking goes, how can you possibly serve our clients well without a similar sacrifice? This is thinking at the most implicit level, but it may dominate how senior generations perceive calls for change.

Understanding feedback as a critical career development tool

There is also a disconnect between the feedback Millennials seek and the responses that Boomers and Xers provide. Millennials often see senior generations as inept in providing useful information when assigning work and helpful feedback at completion.

But that is not how Boomers and Xers perceive it. They see themselves as overworked partners whose capacity to manage client responsibilities and their law firms are stretched too thin. They want those coming into the workplace to understand the level of dedication and commitment it took to get to this point. Moreover, they see a changing profession that leaves little room to do anything other than continue at an even faster pace to accomplish more.

They also recall starting out with little direction or support. "Figure it out" was their mantra and the way that Boomers and Xers succeeded. They built careers by figuring things out, but did so on a firm foundation from their childhood and teen years when they were similarly left on their own to make decisions ranging from how to spend their time to the colleges they would attend.

They also grew up before parents became managers, a transition that, ironically, Boomers and Gen X master-engineered in raising their own children. What they have never understood, however, is the way in which their loving engagement ultimately affected the diminished career navigation skills of Millennials that is at the source of much of the intergenerational tension.

As a generation that received advice throughout their lives from parents, teachers, and coaches, Millennials reasonably expected that the workplace would provide guidance and reactions to their work product in a similarly timely and helpful manner. Law firms, however, too often dismissed the desire for a constructive response as unnecessary hand-holding in an overly-busy work environment.

The reality is that if Boomers and Gen Xers want subsequent generations to have the skills, confidence, and expertise needed to attract and retain clients, ongoing feedback and meaningful evaluations will be an essential component of talent development. Annual reviews that serve as the primary opportunity to offer feedback – and that are often delivered by people unfamiliar with an associate's work – should become an antiquated relic of the past. Developing talent must become a team endeavor where ongoing interaction and feedback is the norm.

Gen X's challenge

Baby Boomers and Gen Xers have seen enormous changes since they began practicing. They are now senior members of firms where offices may be spread throughout regions or around the globe, and where knowing the names of all the people in their practice groups can be a challenge.

Gen Xers, however, face a particularly sensitive challenge in the intergenerational transfer of leadership that is occurring. Their predecessors, the Baby Boomers, found identity in their careers and built workplaces to match their capacity to stay in the game. Retirement felt anathema to a cohort that believed themselves indispensable to their firm's success. Facing a life expectancy far longer than past generations could imagine, retirement may loom more as a necessity than a choice.

That leaves Gen X in the most delicate of positions. And just as in other aspects of their lives, it is one they are expected to manage without fanfare or support.

It will fall to Gen X to help Boomers define their legacy and leave the workplace with grace and a willingness to transfer their knowledge and their client base. In most firms, departing partners have the ultimate power of nurturing the relationship between their clients and their firm, or maintaining control until the day they leave, indifferent to what happens next. This can be a difficult client development challenge that will be dependent on the extent to which Xers are able to manage the process with dignity.

At the same time, Gen X will need to help Millennials step into leadership roles earlier than Xers had to in their careers. There simply are not a sufficient number of Gen Xers to fill the void that will be left as Boomers exit the profession.

They also will need to prepare for Gen Z. Smart strategic planning should anticipate that this generation may have a more difficult transition, especially if the disruptions to their education and opportunities continue indefinitely due to COVID-19.

All of this means that Gen X must undertake the difficult task of managing multiple transitions with sensitivity, a challenge that is rarely discussed. Their own legacy, however, will ultimately depend on how well they navigate this transitional moment.

Changing the rules of engagement

The legal profession has suffered for years from the weight of its own baggage. There is no shortage of articles, books, studies, and speeches that have focused on ways that law firms could create a more flexible, diverse, respectful, and engaged culture. Additional articles and studies demonstrate that these qualities improve the bottom line.

The pandemic has shone a light on many aspects of the legal workplace that can and should be changed. It has also complicated the way in which firms are able to generate new work and new clients. Moving forward into an uncertain future warrants a multi-generational commitment to meet these challenges.

A strategic path forward is to engage all generations in planning for the necessary skills and expertise that law firms will need to retain talent and attract and retain clients. Law firms will function more smoothly if senior generations talk openly about these challenges and bring their younger cohorts into the planning process.

Particularly with respect to the generation of new business, firms should create multi-generational task forces to help devise innovative solutions to existing and anticipated challenges. By empowering younger generations to engage in problem-solving, firms will also deepen the bonds that inevitably emerge when people work together on mutual goals.

Building relationships of trust in the workplace requires a willingness to invest time in each other. Boomers and Xers have an opportunity to change the outdated narrative and create a new, shared reality. The beneficiary of these efforts will include a strengthened and more productive workplace and a more sustainable future.

These conversations should begin today.

Chapter 9:
Homeworking in the new legal ecosystem – the new norm?

By Clare Harman Clark, Taylor Wessing

For many legal businesses, the impact of COVID-19 has been felt most powerfully as a forcible shove into a new world of homeworking. As an accelerator, the pandemic has opened the gates to a new way of working that was perhaps already coming our way. But are we really ready to close the doors on the office? Many lawyers are currently finding that it's less a case of working from home, more living at work – but the touted benefits of flexibility and balance are still tantalizing. If the future of work is to make the very most of this chance to rebase our working lives closer to home, is it truly possible to find a way of replicating digitally the collaboration and inspiration of the office that we miss out on at home?

In retrospect, 2020 was an impromptu experiment in homeworking that no one could ever have hoped to have planned. Of course, many law firms had already embraced the concept of certain employees working remotely; however, virtually overnight, whole law offices across the world emptied as entire workforces stayed home. Overall, the success of this experiment has been mixed, but while the experience of the last few months alone cannot frame the narrative on homeworking going forward, it is positive that there are still real lessons to be learned as we mull the potential for a wholesale shift in how law firms operate moving forward.

Clearly, many law firms have long seen a societal shift in working patterns lumbering over the horizon; and these were already working hard to enable agile working as a standard employee benefit. In a bid to keep the workforce committed and motivated, a flexible offer is routinely seen as fundamental for firms that want to maintain a competitive edge in the recruitment market. Nonetheless, it is not just about creating a culture or a policy whereby working from home is permissible; to be done properly, it comes at a price, and means strategic investment in agile working processes that takes a triumvirate approach to offering a strategic vision for technological capacity, team building and collaboration, and, with more of an eye on those responsible corporate goals, employee acquisition and retention.

Technological capacity as the "new normal"

Many firms have already made considerable investment in deploying the kind of smart technology that gets home offices as near as possible to the real thing. Others are meanwhile using the acceleration effect of the pandemic to start to future-proof those digital systems and infrastructures. To this end, desktop virtualization products such as Citrix for example enable users to work from an identical desktop and access document management systems seamlessly. Underpinning any corporate strategy, however, there is a point around the equity of access for employees and, therefore, career opportunity. This might mean firms helping to increase the spec of an individual's kit, perhaps with the offer of technology loans, or other support for employees to enhance their home connectivity.

Technology can meanwhile be used to create nimble and accessible repositories of knowledge, to enable access to precedent templates, or learning, or present up-to-date analysis of the law. Shifting A4 folders online is no mean feat, but one of the most challenging areas for technology is in shifting to digital learning and training. In many industries, but especially in a law firm, juniors rely on the osmotic learning of keeping one ear open towards a more experienced roommate, but this is virtually impossible without maintaining an open conference call. Designing and packaging virtual training programs are therefore a priority for many firms, but developing a bank of online training and learning sessions requires strategic decision-making on which products firms should use for what purpose.

Podcasts, webinars, virtual roundtables and online presentations are all possibilities for keeping a widely distributed workforce informed, but the effective use of each of these tools after a labor-intensive set-up relies, arguably, on a firm already understanding the preferences and capacities of all parts of its workforce. We already know that people learn in different ways. In fact, trainers point to seven learning styles – visual, aural, verbal, physical, logical, social, and solitary. Some employees might therefore pick up new concepts more easily when they are presented in a spatial or diagrammatic form, for example, while others would prefer to read a book. This breakdown is now overlaid with new consequence. Auditory learners attuned to signals such as pitch or tone might well miss delicate nuances in an online presentation. People accustomed to attending a physical seminar in the office to hear about legal updates might be less inclined to listen to a static podcast in their kitchen. Those who enjoy a nimble discussion round table to learn might have difficulty speaking in an online forum or dropping typed questions into a chat window, particularly if the session is recorded. Conference calls theoretically enable increased diversity, providing a levelling platform for those from different backgrounds, although in practice most are dominated by a few key voices. Even presenting online training is a new challenge for those used to checking the whites of an audience's eyes for understanding.

This training example points to agile workers necessarily acquiring wholly new skillsets, as home working means the day job shifts to accommodate new ways of working. "Train the trainer" strategies might now involve specific learning and development to support the managers and trainers of remotely located teams. The impact of the pandemic has already shown that a fair amount of this will involve adapting our processes and learning, instinctively, on the job; however, it highlights the fact that by shifting working home, we are also shifting the fundamental expectations of our jobs. In the long-term, law firms just like any others will prize digital skillsets when recruiting.

Virtual team-building and collaboration

Many workers have long known that uninterrupted working from home can dramatically improve productivity especially where, for example, they are focused on detailed drafting or writing up an individual project. Still, having made the investment in the technology and practical tools to enable agile working, maximizing its impact really depends on how firms are able to retain the power and the inventiveness of teamwork. Sharing office space is well understood to be crucial for generating ideas and trust; those accidental water cooler encounters are credited with driving inspiration at all levels. How well-equipped are we really to collaborate virtually? And with so many platforms available, there is a chance that valuable contributions fall between the gaps.

Remote working and collaboration may be hot topics in the wake of the pandemic but many platforms have been in development for a long time, and many lawyers have been engaging with off-the-shelf tools for a while with mixed success. Until now, the goal was mostly to reduce cumbersome email traffic, while users still fell back on the reliability of face-to-face meetings in the physical world. Arguably, the communication and emotional nuance in those interactions (often so crucial in client meetings and transaction negotiations) has still not been adequately replicated for teams online, but the software offers range from spaces to chat with instant messaging or video conferencing, to aggregated news feeds, to full-blown project management functionality, and these do clearly assist with much in-house team management. Slack is well-heard of, popular with users for its message search and many integrations of other tools like Trello, which focuses on simple-to-use workflow management. Cisco's WebEx offers personalized video meeting rooms, while Google Docs and Sheets services have their own collaboration tools to allow teams to edit files at the same time. Virtually endemic products such as Microsoft Teams, Zoom and Skype each have their own limitations, and different firms have their own strict standards for security, for obvious reasons. Many firms are still on a fast-moving learning curve when it comes to the multiple features on offer, usability and compatibility with existing systems; it might well be some time before we have an industry consensus on a clear frontrunner.

Clearly there are operational benefits to preserving teamwork, but underpinning this drive to replicate teams virtually is an understanding of the symbiotic balance at the heart of a successful work life – workers who are happy, energized, and supported are also more productive. Many firms have introduced programs for mentoring and coaching team members, rewarding good role models. Firms are also well-advised to consider the clubs and common interests of their workforces, using technology to replicate the shared experiences that bring employees together and help them stay positive and functioning as a team. Virtual team quizzes, yoga, or choir sessions underpin bonds between workers – they also satisfy the need of many responsible firms to understand and deliver on wellness in the workplace, wherever that is.

Employee retention – preserving the work/life balance

It is too simplistic to assume that simply enabling agile working allows firms to tick box their aspirations for being a responsible employer. Talent acquisition and retention is big business and, if anything, the pandemic has shown that a one-size-fits-all approach to working patterns is dangerous. Of course, at the outset of the pandemic, not all firms benefited from a fully-fledged homeworking strategy being already in place, but despite best intentions, learning-by-necessity rather than design has meant that lockdown homeworking has been, for plenty of people, less about working from home, and more about living at work.

This was rarely more obvious than in one major pandemic eye-opener, when countless video calls literally showcased the biggest challenge for working parents – their children. What closed schools lost, conference calls discovered. However, once the novelty of sharing airtime with mini-mes wore off, what remained for many was a rather stressful suspicion that it was no longer possible to effectively segregate work/life space and responsibilities. Firms taking this fear seriously looked to understand the nuances of individual circumstances and help parents adapt, both during the national lockdown and into a new school term with the threat of ongoing localized lockdowns. It's a far cry from the decades-old office culture whereby children could at best be seen on occasional desk photos but ideally not heard.

Similarly, countless other workers have lived through lockdown with other undesirable home circumstances. Those without established home offices were routinely balancing laptops on the couch, whilst those flat-sharing were forced to negotiate the use of quiet corners with flat mates also trying to put in a productive eight hours. The co-living model of smaller private space as against larger communal areas looks particularly problematic in this context. Firms that support agile working in the truest sense appreciate that some projects can be completed out of standard office hours without compromising on client service.

It's working, but not as we know it

When it comes to recovering from the shock of this sudden homeworking experiment, it is interesting to see how some firms are thinking more broadly and creatively when it comes to directing investment towards and articulating the benefits of agile working and workplace segmentation. Indeed, with one eye on workforce sustainability and social responsibility, plenty of law firms have even quickly revolutionized their approach to decision-making here. They are undertaking direct listening exercises with staff, to really understand how their employees feel about the agile working opportunities now on the table. And they are mapping these results against a productivity analysis and no small amount of intuition, when it comes to understanding how the practice of law might better serve employees and clients moving forward.

One likely option for the future clearly seems to lie in an accelerated introduction of agile working across the board. For all the challenges discussed above, it remains the case that plenty of people would seem to welcome a more permanent change to their traditional working patterns, either in terms of a wholesale shift home or at least towards a more agile approach to the working week. A change is as good as a rest, after all. Tendencies for office presenteeism have always raised skeptical eyebrows, and many are now able to justifiably argue that they work just as hard at home as in the office, if not harder. They have actual lived evidence that it's easier to concentrate at home, without demands for chat, or ringing phones. Of course, with reduced attendance at the main office it may mean that certain days attract premium demand for desk space, or increased kudos since senior partners are likely to be in attendance. The pressure is on for firms to manage this appropriately.

Not only has the pandemic proved that it is broadly possible for almost any desk-based role to be based away from an urban head office, it has also had an interesting consequence from an individual employee perspective. Home working has saved considerable commuter costs, both in terms of cash and that greater modern commodity, time. At some point, most people selecting a place to call home are usually forced to undertake a mental calculation of commute time versus anticipated career opportunities and salary. But without the absolute need for daily, lengthy commutes, those same people are now engaging with their lived-in localities; the same ones that they previously only passed through for most of the week. They are changing their relationships with these built environments, exploring neighboring green spaces or buying coffees from independent café businesses rather than a city center multiple. Indeed, many property commentators suggest that this shift couldn't have come at a better time to save beleaguered high streets across the country. It also offers a positive for the environment, in cutting down on business travel. Longer term, it certainly seems fair to assume that office geography will be less constrained and greenbelts will expand as people trade a different way of living for a longer commute when it can be undertaken on fewer workdays.

Elsewhere, the notion of *near* working is also gathering pace. This amounts to a new sort of local working. Rather than rely on home offices exclusively for the new normal, city center firms that are able to undertake workforce location analysis might be able to identify less traditional locations that offer scope for smaller, cheaper, more convenient office satellites. It's hard to imagine that this approach would ever adequately compensate for the loss of a high quality, centrally-located head office, but there may be real advantages for the practice of law, not least during the pandemic.

This would turn existing corporate real estate strategies into a sort of "hub-and-spoke" approach, creating secondary office hubs in areas with high volumes of white-collar workers. Theoretically, this might bring back some of the real-world benefits of in-person collaboration and innovation, and position agile working as a catalyst for structural change that reinvigorates our towns, although clearly its success is highly dependent on many complex factors, not least ensuring a critical mass of employees and a flexible approach to contracting for space.

Conclusion

Of course, a permanent shift to the way we work relies on more than identifying the challenges highlighted during the pandemic and finding ways to adapt to overcome these. Fundamentally, it relies on the appetite of businesses leaders. The coronavirus is going nowhere fast, but the support and commitment of leaders will need to be channeled into agile working strategies; then clearly and consistently communicated in order to empower and equip managers and teams to fully benefit. Only this way might the legal ecosystem reap the benefits of agile working beyond the immediate reactionary lockdown and into a positive, and strategically-planned, future – pandemic or not.

Chapter 10: Why being more human and crafting connections with staff will deliver results

By Chris Marston, chief executive, LawNet

Leading a law firm in today's shifting landscape demands agility and a willingness to cope with uncertainty. Resilience is essential and tight financial management crucial, but perhaps most important is the need to engage and enthuse employees through these unprecedented times.

Change management has always been a challenge, but where we used to measure change in months and years, in 2020, it has been measured in hours and days. Each of us was forced to experience and absorb rapid adjustments as the pandemic gripped the world, reaching into every aspect of our personal and working lives.

From the outset we found ourselves engulfed in a crisis management situation without a playbook; we had no *Harvard Business Review* tips pinned to the wall on how to lead through a pandemic. We had to figure things out, largely on our own, and at speed. The pace, quality and authenticity of the response to such extreme circumstances can determine which firms will succeed and demands flexibility and vision from leaders.

LawNet's response

During lockdown we initiated a series of weekly themed conversations between the leaders of the mid-size law firms that comprise our 70-strong member network, also drawing in expert guest contributors to join our live video sessions. From the outset, firms were reporting how the crisis had driven new change programs or accelerated greatly some existing modernization plans. Suddenly all those ideas around agile working, paperless projects and video conferencing had assumed a sense of urgency. This crash-landed into an environment that was already fast-moving, one where law firms were being challenged to adapt with alacrity.

Much of the innovation has been in the use of digital solutions, with widespread adoption of online channels for internal and external meetings now commonplace, but such technological advancement cannot fully replace true human connection. Employees have fundamental psychological needs that must be met if they are to be successful and collaborative in their roles, whether they are working together in the office or remotely, connected only by the internet.

Before the pandemic, we could already see employees seeking more than simply a salary. They wanted purpose and meaning, they needed strong relationships in the workplace, they wanted to be coached to the next level. That is no less important now, but people's working lives carry greater fragility. As furlough, redundancy, and the threat of recession combined to undermine confidence and cloud the future in the earlier months of the pandemic, so loyalties continue to be tested in new ways with the opportunities for staff seeking different lifestyles beyond the nine-to-five commute. The attraction of working from a rural or suburban home, instead of commuting to work from a small flat in the city, may seem hard to resist.

These factors reinforce the importance of excellent employee engagement, whether navigating through the pandemic or looking ahead to the long haul, with research showing organizations with actively engaged employees outperform across the board.

Recent meta-analysis by Gallup[1] revealed higher sales, productivity and profitability, combined with lower staff turnover, for those businesses featuring in the top quartile for employee engagement. It is an essential pre-requisite for delivering enhanced performance and maintaining a sharp competitive edge. As such, maintaining a truly engaged and motivated workforce should be the top priority for leaders, regardless of the challenges or threats that may be encountered.

Challenging thinking

We want to build collaborative, committed teams and for that we need effective employee engagement. But how will we do that in a post-COVID world when agile working is likely to be part of the new normal for the foreseeable future? New approaches will be vital to ensure engagement if people are working outside traditional office structures, with those working from home some or all of the time more vulnerable to feeling socially isolated.

Globally, it has been estimated that 85 percent of employees do not feel actively engaged at work.[2] This was before the pandemic, and future research will inform us whether the new ways of working introduced during lockdown periods have seen this percentage improve or deteriorate. Either way, that is still a lot of disengaged people at work every day. Why is it so hard to get the team on board?

Defining the metric

While many organizations implement some sort of employee engagement program or check the lie of the land through regular surveying, few get it right, even when they take follow-up actions to try and improve low scores. Leaders may blame the tool, the measurement, their own demographic or environmental factors, but few identify that the failure is more likely to lie in the way their employee engagement program has been executed.

The metric may be too complicated, it may be outside the control of managers, or it may not relate to the psychological needs of employees. The questions could be too selective, ignoring the problems that lie in their blind spot, resulting in apparently high engagement scores without correspondingly strong performance outcomes. Some surveys ask the right questions but fail to follow through or respond adequately to the feedback received.

Most importantly, employee engagement will not succeed where ownership of the process and its outcomes is not grasped by leaders; too often it is considered to be the role of HR, something separate from the rest of organizational life, or simply viewed as a tactical check list.

Surveys have a place, but as an instrument for change, not an end in themselves. If the result of a survey is a change in the conversations managers have, or to enable or encourage different behaviors in the organization, then it is performing a useful role. Just accepting the results and filing them away for comparison next year is not.

However, where engagement is integrated into the business strategy, and used as a performance lever, it can generate significant gains. Great managers recognize that engagement is their prime responsibility, and one that can differentiate their own performance when the focus is on being a coach, not a boss.

This is borne out by Gallup's research, which shows that employees who receive daily feedback and interaction with their manager are three times more likely to be engaged than those who receive little or no development input during the year.

Feedback is an essential component of staff development, but it should be part of an ongoing, positive coaching conversation, not an annual critique. Too often it is channeled through the appraisal process, or "performance review", and in such a situation is more likely to spark the same emotional response in the human brain as someone approaching you from behind in a dark alley, shutting down the receptors you want to ignite.

Some of the most important defining characteristics of good employee engagement involve ensuring individuals know the value of their work, how it contributes to the organization, that their role is acknowledged, and that they are given opportunities to grow. Workplace culture is complex and there are no quick fixes, but leaders and managers can make their interactions with their people more meaningful by providing frequent recognition of contribution, making sure people feel the organization cares about them, and that their opinions count.

Employees cannot be innovators and the organization cannot be agile and creative unless there are clear expectations and permission to experiment.

Crafting the conversation

Opening up the dialogue so people feel heard and valued is vital. Within our own organization we have taken on board the principles espoused by Dr Tim Baker and his Five Conversations Framework.[3] He developed this as an alternative to the potentially damaging appraisal process, which too often turns into an infrequent box ticking process and a monologue rather than the conversation it needs to be.

Baker proposed regular themed conversations involving everyone within the organization to give an organizational snapshot. These are focused on the individual and what areas of support they may need, their experience within the organization, and to invite ideas for improvements that could benefit them, their team, and the organization as a whole. By taking the temperature in this way, problems can be identified and solutions sought.

Our experience of this approach is that it is far less stressful than any traditional form of appraisal and helps build better relationships between team members, while allowing us to identify and build upon individual strengths.

It is important for leaders to be ready to adapt and improve, even the things that are working well, and in adopting new ideas such as this, one should not be prescriptive. Within LawNet HQ we have fine-tuned our own version of the themed conversations framework to make it better suited to our own profile.

Similarly, one of our member firms has described how they have adapted Baker's approach to better match their firm, with just three themed conversations – training and development, climate review, and innovation and growth. They are also flexible in allowing the conversations to go off topic, if more pressing matters arise during the review. Reporting on the success of the approach, they say, "We see staff who have been with us a long time, and who were on record as having considered appraisals a bit of a waste of time, putting thought into the specific topics and coming back with good ideas".

As ever in business, there will be winners and losers ahead, but to have any chance of winning we must embrace change, harness the energy and talents of our people by motivating and engaging them, and focus on the exciting potential that offers for the future.

Great workplaces do not happen by accident, nor do they grow without nurture. It takes flexibility, an openness to new ideas, regular and honest communication, and buy-in from employees at every level. Perhaps most important is recognizing that by being more human, we can make the difference and help unleash the potential of our people – the beating heart of any business strategy.

Enhancing engagement – some practical examples

Leaders who listen

Leadership style is the foundation stone for great employee relationships. We need to create an environment where we place trust in our people and enable them to build on their strengths. As law firm strategist Andrew Hedley urged when he joined our leaders' forum in the guest slot, firms must capitalize on the responsive, flexible approach they have proved themselves capable of during 2020, and leaders should adopt a *challenge and support* philosophy, rather than *command and control*.

This latter style tends to run in tandem with an attitude of presenteeism and rule-keeping, which can be particularly negative when staff are supporting a philosophy of agile working. Encouraging behavioral change in leaders and managers is important if they are to develop good listening and coaching skills. The ability to make that shift may need to be taught and a stronger coaching culture across the whole business can support such development.

Research suggests that individual managers can account for as much as 70 percent of the variance in team engagement, because they have such a pivotal role in ensuring that employees know what work they must do, supporting them where necessary and showing how their work contributes to the organization as a whole. This makes access to good learning and development at all levels crucial to good engagement and even more so in the current working environment. Funds that were previously directed at entertaining or externally-run courses can usefully be diverted into soft skills development. Certainly, this is a shift we anticipate and have already moved towards virtual delivery of our management and leadership skills program, following on from our legal update courses which went online in April, once lockdown prevented physical attendance.

Handling emotions

The speed and force of change during the early days of the pandemic meant that individuals faced numerous new and uncomfortable situations in quick succession, with little chance to process before dealing with the next curve ball. Inevitably, handling this cataclysmic change may have translated into fear, frustration or anger – emotions that are often recorded during times of transition. While the initial denial and frustration of individuals is likely to follow the usual path of exploration and acceptance in due course, it may take time to work itself out.

Similarly, where new ways of working may have been accepted initially, by both staff and clients, these may become irksome when it becomes the everyday. Reports of video call fatigue or a general despondency and desire to get "back to normal" all add to the difficulty of keeping people engaged.

We have seen plenty of creative and open-minded initiatives from firms, such as offering staff greater flexibility, or setting up social interactions such as quiz nights, increasing communication through video messaging tools, and using surveys to invite feedback, but no single idea can be a panacea for bringing teams through the pandemic. There's no silver bullet, no vaccine to guarantee immunity from dissatisfaction and disenfranchisement, particularly when a "them and us" attitude might have developed over furloughing.

Workers may be doing too many hours in difficult circumstances and feeling irritated to see others at home being "paid to do nothing". Those at home could feel dispensable, anxious at being left with nothing to do, and feeling equally challenged. Mental health and wellbeing are paramount and communicating to all staff that leaders recognize the situation and value them as individuals is essential.

Dr Brian Marien is an expert in how our brains work and how we handle stress and uncertainty, and has presented to LawNet's network over recent years. He argues in a recent webinar[4] that in this unique era of uncertainty, prioritizing psychological health has become crucial for organizational survival. Preliminary findings suggest that the prevalence of anxiety alone has more than doubled. This has serious implications for both our wellbeing and our performance, affecting individuals and organizations alike. He points to the importance of evidence-based tools and "protective factors" that can help to increase our tolerance of uncertainty, reduce anxiety, and enable us to fulfil our potential, even in these turbulent times.

Creative ideas to tackle problems head on and bring the firm together can be vital at this time. For example, some of our member firms tried a rolling program of furlough across different groups of staff, so that the burden could be shared. Another firm is building a bonus pot to reward all team members, but with special consideration for those who have gone above and beyond during this time. The idea has been well received, but managers were careful to canvass options with staff to be sure it was going to have the intended outcome – motivated, committed teams are not grown in the dark.

When it comes to redundancy, consider dealing with this earlier rather than later. People are anxious about the future, and certainty on this front can be better for everyone in the organization. Uncertainty and worry can be more damaging for people than the concrete knowledge that their job has gone. It may seem a good idea to delay that difficult conversation with those you know will be let go once furlough ends, but those whose jobs are safe could be reassured, resulting in improved performance.

Understanding staff

Taking time to understand individual staff in a holistic way can help redefine organizational purpose. Recognizing how their work and home lives are inter-related, and how you might help them be more fulfilled in both spheres, can have a meaning way beyond the purely operational level. The traditional office environment provides a social purpose in bringing people together in one place. Obviously, that has been missing in recent months and some may value being first to come back to the office if they are feeling isolated working alone. For others, progress may be a more flexible daily home-working routine or only being in the office certain days of the week. Leaders must create within their firms a social purpose as well as a business purpose, and an enhanced employee value proposition, while also fulfilling the objective of keeping the business agile and profitable.

Some of that may come through greater inclusivity. More than half of new entrants to the legal profession are female[5] but their skills, talent, and experience are often ignored once they leave to start a family. The career break may mean they have to re-skill and retrain when they return and could feel disadvantaged because they have not advanced their career at the same pace as others. More agile working in the current situation opens the door to harnessing these talents and engaging with a valuable, under-utilized section of the workforce.

Similarly, greater flexibility in working hours, enabling a more responsive attitude towards client-facing interaction, can bring benefits to the organization while enabling staff to balance personal and work commitments. Client expectations have changed just as dramatically over the past few months, and it makes sense to match these going forward.

Rewriting the rules

We must empower and delegate, but in doing so we must be quite clear about what we expect from our staff, so they know the shape and extent of their responsibilities. In this "new normal", it is important to revisit this and develop a framework for people if they are not in the office, to agree what that means and what it looks like.

This was the focus for another of our guest experts – Robert Camp, formerly a managing partner at Stephens Scown and now working with law firms in strategic innovation. Things are not as they were, so where everyone may have been expected to take their lunch hour at lunchtime when they were in the office, that may not fit with the flexibility they need if working at home and balancing personal issues such as childcare or opportunities to interact with others to avoid de-socialization.

For example, during lockdown everyone was encouraged to take exercise every day, and that is a good habit to continue, but is there a restriction on when that may be taken? Must it be taken at lunchtime or do we want to encourage staff to take it when they want to, with the resulting uplift in productivity.

In this context, asking people how they are feeling and what they are thinking – on a personal, one-on-one basis – is an important step forward. It's perhaps best undertaken by line managers, in a safe environment where people feel confident in speaking out, as HR may now be perceived as the four horsemen of the apocalypse, having been the conduit for furlough, pay cuts, short time and redundancy.

References

1. Gallup's perspective on building a high-development culture through your employee engagement strategy, Gallup Inc, 2019.
2. www.gallup.com/workplace/231668/dismal-employee-engagement-sign-global-mismanagement.aspx
3. *The End of the Performance Review: A New Approach to Appraising Employee Performance*, Tim Baker, 2013.

4. Dr Brian Marien, The Positive Group: www.positivegroup.org/profile/dr-brian-marien/
5. Law Society www.lawgazette.co.uk/law/it-was-100-years-ago-today-profession-marks-opening-to-women/5102587.article

Chapter 11: The logistical and human challenges of the pandemic – a case study

By Chris Boyd, Allison Blixt, and Jullia Carretta, Wilson Sonsini Goodrich & Rosati

How did we, as a firm, remain connected when we went from 16 offices to more than 1,600 virtual offices, essentially overnight? How could we keep our people healthy and engaged?

This case study details how we have taken a multi-pronged, collaborative, cross-department approach to address the myriad challenges associated with this new working world, which included moving everyone virtual; communicating and managing across 1,600 virtual offices; maintaining wellbeing when work and home life merge; and connecting with colleagues and clients. Underlying all of these is a focus on supporting our diverse employees and developing additional diversity and inclusion (D&I) initiatives.

We outline below what we have been doing over the past few months in the hope that other law firms and legal service organizations may find this information useful as they manage remote attorney recruiting, professional development, employee engagement, and D&I programs. We would be happy to discuss any of these items in more detail, as we are all navigating these changing times.

Moving all talent development virtual

In mid-March, once we issued a firm-wide work-from-home order, we faced the challenge of moving almost all existing employees to a virtual environment, including those who previously only worked in-person, in a firm office, with a desktop computer. Our IT department worked tirelessly to get everyone set up with the right tools and to offer support with this transition.

We also had to move all new employee orientation virtual within four working days. This was no small task and required significant collaboration between various departments, including professional development,

IT, attorney recruiting, human resources and office managers. Of course, most of the people involved from these teams had also just moved to virtual working and were navigating this as individuals.

Our priority was to make the onboarding process as smooth as possible for the new hires who were joining in a time of such uncertainty. We wanted to ensure communication was as clear as possible to avoid any confusion, especially on their first day with the firm. Leading this process, the professional development team's other priority was to streamline our communication with presenters across the firm. We needed to make sure everyone understood their role, knew "where" to be and when, and understood how to use the relevant technology from their own "new offices". We reached out to each presenter individually to discuss all of this and test the technology. Many people had never set up video meetings themselves and were now being asked to do this, while working remotely. Our regional IT coordinators saved the day more than once in helping make all of this come together.

In late February, as concerns about COVID-19 escalated across the globe, we were faced with the question of what to do about our annual academies for first, third, fifth, and seventh year associates (luckily our new partner program had taken place in February). These academies are multiday, offsite events that associates from across all our offices usually attend in-person. The academies are important milestone gatherings that help associates in a class year connect, learn what success looks like at the next level, and build skills to help them succeed at that level. Our Third Year Academy (3YA) was scheduled to take place in the San Francisco Bay Area in mid-March. Initially, we considered holding a program for only local associates, thinking it would be better to do an in-person event for some people rather than nothing.

It quickly became apparent that any type of in-person event would be impossible, as we issued firm-wide restrictions on firm gatherings and travel. Again, collaborating and communicating were fundamental. We knew associates would be disappointed and worried about missing a critical career development and networking opportunity, so we wanted to reassure them that we would be going ahead at a later date. We worked with our travel department to cancel everyone's travel plans centrally. We negotiated with the hotel hosting the event to postpone to August (looking back, we have to appreciate our optimism). We began a similar process (of postponing) the Fifth Year Academy, initially scheduled for late April.

Over the next weeks, as the gravity of the situation became apparent, we realized we were not going to be going ahead with any in-person events for the foreseeable future. We had to change tack. Could we make these events work virtually? What could that look like?

In the meantime, we had been working with the attorney recruiting team to find ways to make a virtual summer program work. The priorities were to ensure the health and safety of everyone involved and to provide a valuable summer experience. We decided to hold a shortened six-week, virtual program from 15 June until 24 July and to give each of the incoming summer associates an offer to join the firm as a fall associate in 2021. Consistent with our commitment to providing pro bono legal services, we gave the option to earn the six weeks' summer associate salary by performing six weeks of legal work for a 501(c)(3) qualified nonprofit of their choice. We also gave the opportunity to spend a week or two of the summer program doing online certification programs offered by the Berkeley Center for Law and Business. When these plans were announced, the attorney recruiting team held a webinar with the incoming summer associates and were available afterward via email or phone to address any individual's questions or concerns.

Making the summer program work remotely required collaboration across the firm and with external providers. We engaged InsideSherpa (now Forage), a virtual work experience platform, to help build online modules and resources to supplement what we were designing internally. We used online videoconferencing to host events, including training classes, panels, and social gatherings. We created working groups across offices for a virtual team project. Work was allocated through our usual online system, slightly adapted to the virtual environment. We included the summer associates in affinity group meetings, described below. We wanted the summer associates to feel as connected to and supported by the firm as they would in a "normal" summer. The feedback on the program was overwhelmingly positive, although of course many summer associates reported missing the in-person element. One summer associate shared:

> *"Overall, this summer was way more than I could have hoped for. I got to meet many people, do interesting and exciting work, and learn about the firm. It was a good time, though very busy (which is also good!)"*

Back to the associate academies. In mid-May, we emailed all our lawyers about the associate academies going ahead virtually. We knew we would do it, we just didn't know exactly how. Several partners and other leaders reached out right away offering help, one of many examples of how supportive our people have been during these challenging times. We scheduled the academies to run monthly, starting with 3YA in August, giving us enough time to plan and a reasonable amount of time in between each of them (it seemed reasonable at the time!). Early on, we knew we couldn't (and didn't want to) ask the associates (or ourselves) to sit in front of a screen for a full day, or even a substantial part of the day. We planned to spread each academy out over a week of daily two- to three-hour slots. Historically, feedback from our academies has shown that, unsurprisingly, one of the most valuable aspects is connecting with associates from other offices and practice groups. We wanted to find a way to create connection in a virtual environment. As we had used video conferencing for some smaller scale classes and for the summer program, we planned to use it for 3YA as well, allowing the option to use both random and pre-assigned break-out rooms of any size.

Specifically, we included facilitated speed networking in small, random break-out rooms to build connection. We also pre-allocated associates to "3YA pods", break-out groups we would use throughout the academy. We allocated these pods to be regional, based on feedback from the summer program that being allocated a group across time zones made things unnecessarily difficult. The pods proved popular, and we are encouraging associates to stay connected with their pod in the weeks and months ahead.

The program included sessions covering business development, management, Q&A with our managing partner, presentation skills, and more. We used subject matter experts from within the firm and liaised with them on creating their virtual sessions. We found various ways to make sessions interactive – using the chat feature, polling, changing screen names in response to a prompt, using break-out rooms for small group discussion and then returning with a question per group, etc. Despite being virtual, associates appreciated the opportunity to connect with their colleagues from other offices.

> *"I enjoyed getting to know my colleagues (and realizing what a great group they were) and also got a lot out of the management training session."*

> *"[The highlight was] meeting other third years, especially firm-wide. It was comforting to know that people are going through some of the same things you are. It also presents opportunities to collaborate across departments in the future."*

To facilitate even more interactivity, we are testing a platform for future academies and other events that would allow attendees to join a "table" during breaks, not just break-out rooms during the sessions. This could provide another way to connect that wouldn't be as forced as being sent to a random or PD-allocated break-out room. We hope to pilot this platform at the Seventh Year Academy in October and perhaps also use it at our Women's Leadership Summit in December to provide virtual networking opportunities.

Keeping everyone connected and engaged

As always, but especially in 2020, the importance of communicating effectively and often within teams, across the firm, and with clients, cannot be overstated. Since 17 March, our board chair and our managing partner have been holding regular firm-wide town halls, originally by teleconference, and more recently by video. They provide timely, relevant information about the firm's plans, finances, and initiatives and responses to questions submitted in advance. These have been very well-received and appreciated throughout the crises of 2020. Our board chair and our managing partner, with representatives from relevant administrative support teams, have also been holding regular calls with the Associates' Committee to respond to their questions and concerns and meeting with the partner Culture Committee to address challenges and find solutions together.

In March, representatives from our professional development, career development, community affairs, and HR teams formed Team Engage to encourage wellbeing and connection across the firm. This team launched a weekly, firm-wide engagement email and an associated intranet page under the banner "Stay Healthy. Stay Connected. Stay Engaged." Through this initiative, we have provided various tips and suggestions, shared links to resources and internal and external classes, highlighted personal stories, held regular photo and caption competitions, offered ideas for team-building, and provided information about relevant employee benefits. The content is also shared on the intranet page, including photo contest winners and honorable mentions. We have received responses and submissions from across teams, roles, and offices. We have appreciated pictures of dramatic landscapes, new quarantine hairstyles and random online purchases. We have celebrated graduations and the start of school. We have enjoyed artistic creations and wonderful recipes for ice cream and BBQ extravaganzas. Feedback for the Team Engage initiative has been very positive:

Administrative manager: *"So much great information in here. I really appreciate all that you and the team do to give us ideas to take care of ourselves and each other!"*

Executive assistant: *"I'm so honored to have my pictures featured! Thank you, WSGR Engage Team!"*

Of counsel: *"This was a particularly fun read. Just wanted to share that I enjoyed it!"*

Office supervisor: *"Thank you... for all this information and encouragement. Although I can't always do these things, I know that the resources are available and that alone provides some comfort."*

Partner: *"I just want to say that I LOVE your emails and I read all of them. I think they are very useful for all associates and staff... Just wanted to say thanks for all of your creative ideas and suggestions."*

Supporting diverse employees

Our Diversity and Inclusion Committee (DAIC) membership was finalized in early May and includes partners, associates, firm leadership, and diversity staff. We have representatives from a cross-section of our departments, offices, and all our affinity groups. Getting the DAIC formalized was a critical step to further advancing our D&I initiatives and ensuring people across the firm are aware of what we are planning and can connect with someone if they have suggestions or concerns. We sent a firm-wide email launching the DAIC and providing an update about our ongoing initiatives. We also recently opened all our affinity groups to everyone at the firm – lawyers and staff, those who identify as diverse, and allies. Clearly, inclusion and connection are incredibly important now more than ever. We must all remain conscious of this and the DAIC plays an important role.

Following the tragic killing of George Floyd and the ensuing worldwide protests for racial justice, we held a town hall in early June dedicated to stressing our support for our Black colleagues, clients, and friends. Firm leadership collaborated with leaders of our African American affinity group and the DAIC to ensure that our message encompassed our firm values and amplified the voices of our Black colleagues. We also issued a public statement supporting the Black community and committing to ongoing changes to identify and confront bias and systemic racial injustice.

We held meetings for our African American affinity group to check in on everyone. We also facilitated office meetings, on request, to give people the opportunity to share their feelings, to hear about others' experiences and to support each other. Through the Wilson Sonsini Foundation, we launched a firm-wide matching campaign supporting respected nonprofit organizations focused on racial justice and the fight against discrimination including the Equal Justice Initiative, the Lawyers' Committee for Civil Rights of the San Francisco Bay Area, and the NAACP Legal Defense and Educational Fund.

We recently shared the latest edition of our Diversity and Inclusion newsletter, which provides our colleagues and clients a chance to learn about our ongoing initiatives, such as our recent pledge to increase our pro bono legal services specifically dedicated to racial justice and civil rights work. We have pledged a $15 million dollar increase in our services over the next three years.

In April, we started hosting videoconference affinity group meetings and have held regular virtual meetings since then, including the ones mentioned above. Adding professional staff has aided this sense of community. Many staff members, including some who have been with the firm for decades, have shared that they have never felt so connected, even though they are working remotely. They had never been invited to actively participate in any groups before. Having everyone on video also allows people in any office to connect. It is a great equalizer, as at some point in every call, someone speaks at the same time as someone else, or someone's child cries, or someone's dog barks. It has created a sense of real connection with real people, not with someone in a work costume. We plan to continue using this medium, even when people are back in offices.

Wellbeing and connection

We signed the ABA's wellbeing pledge in 2018 and have taken that pledge to heart. Once we began sheltering in place, our priority was the well-being of our employees and their families. Firm leadership encouraged our department heads, leaders, and managers to check-in with their teams regularly. Our HR, professional development, and D&I teams check-in with each office to ensure those experiencing hardships have the support they need and to provide any additional guidance where our benefit programs can provide resources. Our benefits team has been exploring and introducing new benefits and new ways to access them.

In May, we adapted our plans for our first annual Wilson Sonsini Well-Being Week (mirroring the ABA's Lawyer Well-Being Week) to work virtually. That week's Team Engage emails encouraged everyone to check in on their own and others' wellbeing, our goal being to raise awareness and encourage action to support wellbeing. We included a suggested activity for each day.

- Monday – standing or walking meetings.
- Tuesday – a specified activity to connect with your values.
- Wednesday – a communication class offered by our PD team.
- Thursday – show your gratitude to someone you appreciate.
- Friday – attend a yoga or meditation session offered internally.

We also included information about Mental Health Awareness Month and relevant resources and benefits we offer. We are launching a mental health and wellbeing network in October to help reduce the stigma about mental health challenges and to provide a forum for sharing and supporting each other.

To encourage connection and career development, we also recently relaunched our Associate Mentoring Program. We matched people across offices and practice areas based on a questionnaire exploring what the mentees sought in a mentor and what the mentors could help develop in their mentees. We also offered the option to be matched with someone in a specific affinity group, with specific hobbies or with other common interests. The virtual environment has alleviated invisible barriers that were previously perceived and, through videoconferencing, engagement in the program has increased.

Thus far, 2020 has brought many challenges, but we have managed to find opportunities to build community and keep our people connected and engaged. We have learned some important key lessons along the way.

- Increased communication such as regular firm-wide town halls and weekly engagement emails have been well-received and a version of these will continue beyond COVID-19.
- The videoconferencing and other collaboration tools relied on in the current environment will be incredibly helpful for us going forward.
- Shared challenges have removed some formal barriers that may have existed and have allowed people to connect more casually and should help solidify relationships going forward.
- The importance of flexibility, adaptability, and grace cannot be overstated.

www.ingramcontent.com/pod-product-compliance
Ingram Content Group UK Ltd.
Pitfield, Milton Keynes, MK11 3LW, UK
UKHW021849150926
8657IPUK00005B/151

9 781783 584000